Dean Burgon's 𝕨arnings on Revision

OF
THE TEXTUS RECEPTUS AND THE KING JAMES BIBLE

By Rev. D. A. Waite, Th.D., Ph.D.

the
BIBLE
FOR
TODAY
900 Park Avenue
Collingswood, NJ 08108
Phone: 609-854-4452

B.F.T. #804

Published by

THE BIBLE FOR TODAY PRESS
900 Park Avenue
Collingswood, New Jersey 08108
U.S.A.

July, 1998

Copyright, 1998
All Rights Reserved

ISBN #1-56848-013-X

Dean John William Burgon
(1813–1888)
A Conservative Anglican Minister

ACKNOWLEDGMENTS

I wish to thank and acknowledge the assistance of the following people:

- **Yvonne S. Waite**, my wife, who encouraged the reprinting of the book, read the manuscript, and, as always, gave many helpful suggestions;

- **Daniel S. Waite**, our youngest son, the Assistant to the Bible For Today Director, who offered helpful suggestions, searched successfully for the proper printer, and saw the work through the printing process to final completion.

FOREWORD

- **A Revision of a 1980 Book**. This book was first published on April 15, 1980 under the title: *Dean John Burgon's Prerequisites for Major Revision of the New Testament Greek Textus Receptus and the English King James Version New Testament*. Many have ordered it and read it in the intervening 18 years. The title has been revised to *Dean Burgon's Warnings on Revision of the Textus Receptus and the King James Bible*. I hope many more readers will read this material in this new and improved format.

- **A Great Need**. In this year of 1998, there is still a very great need to understand Dean John William Burgon's **WARNINGS** concerning revision, either of the Greek Textus Receptus or of the King James Bible. Dean Burgon, the master textualist, had some very important **WARNINGS** in his scholarly book, *The Revision Revised*. The Dean Burgon Society has reprinted this fine volume in a 640 page hardback beautiful edition. It is available as **B.F.T. #611 @ $25.00 +$5.00 S&H**. The readers are encouraged to study this book and check out the page references for themselves.

- **When Will the Revisions Cease?** There seems to be no end in sight for the many revisions that have been made, and are still being made both in the Greek New Testament and in the English King James Bible. Most modern publishers and writers have not read what Dean Burgon wrote extensively concerning any revision of the Greek or English Bible. The few who have read his **WARNINGS** have unwisely disregarded them. Though Dean Burgon was an Anglican minister and I am a Baptist minister, our joint-love for the very Words of God have bound us together in a similar cause--*In Defense of Traditional Bible Texts*.

- **Tell Others About this Book.** I trust our readers will help us in the distribution of this book far and wide. It is hoped that many will cease from their desire to change either the Greek or English Bible texts. They should have confidence in the King James Bible and in the Hebrew and Greek texts that underlie it. Until **ALL** of Dean Burgon's **WARNING PREREQUISITES** have been heeded, we must keep the Biblical *status quo*!

Sincerely yours for God's Words,

D. A. Waite

Rev. D. A. Waite, Th.D., Ph.D.
Director, The Bible For Today, Incorporated

THE BIBLE

"Majestic, eternal, immutable BOOK,
Inspired, inerrant, complete.
The Light of my path as I walk on life's way,
The Guide and the Lamp to my feet.

Its writings are holy and verbally true,
The unalterable Statute of Light,
For profit, for doctrine, for correction, reproof,
Infallible Guide to the right.

My Treasure, my Comfort, my Help, and my Stay,
Incomparable Measure and Rod,
Each page is replete with its textual proof,
The Bible, the exact WORD OF GOD!

By Gertrude Grace Sanborn
(1904--1988)

TABLE OF CONTENTS

APPENDIX I
THE LINGUISTIC TRAINING AND QUALIFICATIONS OF SOME OF THE TRANSLATORS OF THE KING JAMES BIBLE OF 1611 71

I.
INTRODUCTORY
CONSIDERATIONS

[Note: This book was first published on April 15, 1980, under the title *Dean John Burgon's Prerequisites for Major Revision of the New Testament Greek Textus Receptus and the English King James Version New Testament.* The present printing has a lot of the same material in it, but with some revisions. Though much has taken place in the eighteen years from 1980 to 1998 in the battle for our Bibles, I believe this study will be especially helpful for many years to come for all who read it and grasp the importance of it. For this reason, it is now being made available in a new and up-dated format. DAW]

A. Why This Book? This is a study of Dean John William Burgon's **WARNINGS** about the revision of the Textus Receptus and the King James Bible. These **WARNINGS** took the form of various prerequisites before there should be any legitimate consideration of a major revision of either the New Testament Greek Textus Receptus or the English King James Bible's New Testament. Here are some of the reasons for this book.

1. Because THE DEAN BURGON SOCIETY Was Organized As of November, 1978. The first reason for this study is because of the organization of THE DEAN BURGON SOCIETY, INCORPORATED, as of November, 1978. As of the present edition of this book, the DBS is twenty years old. This Society is a tax exempt, nonprofit, fundamental Christian corporation, with the present mailing address of Box 354, Collingswood, New Jersey 08108 (Phone: 609-854-4452; FAX: 609-854-2464). The Society bears the name of Dean John William Burgon. It has, as its motto: "IN DEFENSE OF TRADITIONAL BIBLE TEXTS."

The question has been raised by many writers and speakers from November, 1978, until this present date, as to whether or not Dean Burgon would revise in a major fashion either the Greek Textus Receptus, or the English King James Bible New Testament. If the answer is in the affirmative for either the Greek or the English, the next three questions would be **"by whom,"** **"when"** and **"how."** I will attempt to discuss all of these questions in this study. Dean Burgon sounded forth many specific **WARNINGS** about any revision of either the Traditional or Received Text or the Authorized King James Bible.

2.   Because, as President of THE DEAN BURGON SOCIETY, I Was Asked to Speak on this Very Subject at the DBS Annual Meeting, October, 1979. A second reason for this study is because I was asked to speak on this same subject at the First Annual Meeting of THE DEAN BURGON SOCIETY (DBS), which was held in October, 1979, at Watertown, Wisconsin, in the Calvary Baptist Church. It was an important question in 1979, and it is equally important today, especially in view of the many, many revisions that have been made both in the New Testament Greek Text and in the New Testament English text. Having to prepare for that speech, I saw the very important questions and **WARNINGS** which Dean John Burgon raised concerning any revision. He was a master textual student among the conservative Anglican churchmen of his day. He lived from 1813 to 1888. The cassette tape of that speech is one of the seven recorded in the DBS meeting series (**B.F.T. #758/3**). It is available @ **$4.00+S&H.**

3.   Because I Was Asked for a Written Study on This Subject. A third reason for this study is because of a request from Mr. Everett W. Fowler, a member of the DEAN BURGON SOCIETY'S Executive Committee. Mr. Fowler, now with the Lord, was a very careful student of the Greek New Testament and its textual make-up. His important book, *Evaluating the Versions of the New Testament*, is still available. It is **B.F.T. #952 @ $5 + S&H.** He asked if it would be possible to have this taped material in written form for further use and easier distribution to others. I told him that when time permitted, I would do as he requested. This present book is the result.

4.   Because of a Misunderstanding on the Part of Some People Concerning Dean Burgon's Views and A Misquotation of His Position on When He Would Revise the T.R. and K.J.B. I have read some articles which quoted parts of Dean John William Burgon's words on the subject of revision of either the

Received Greek Text or the King James Bible. These articles failed to give Dean Burgon's complete views on this subject. This is unfortunate-- especially when very few people have access to Dean Burgon's books. The books were out of print for many years. The Bible For Today reprinted and made available all five of Dean Burgon's books on this theme in copy- machine format. In recent years, the Dean Burgon Society has reprinted as regular books four of Dean Burgon's books: (1) *The Last Twelve Verses of Mark* in perfect bound format (**B.F.T. #1139 @ $15 + S&H**); (2) *The Revision Revised* in hardback (**B.F.T. #611 @ $25 + S&H**); (3) *The Traditional Text* in hardback (**B.F.T. #1159 @ $16 + S&H**); and (4) *Causes of Corruption of the Traditional Text* in hardback (**B.F.T. #1160 @ $15 + S&H**). It is possible that at its 1998 meeting, the Dean Burgon Society will decide to print as a hardback book, Dean Burgon's *Inspiration and Inter- pretation.* It is hoped that this present study and his excellent books will bring a clearer understanding of Dean John William Burgon's views and **WARNINGS ON REVISION**.

> **5.**   **Because of Such a Rash of Versions, Per- versions, and Translations in English and Such a Num- ber of Revisions of the Greek Textus Receptus.** I am prompted to ask, with Dean John William Burgon, concerning the various English versions and perversions now in existence as well as the various revisions of the New Testament Greek Text, "Are they really necessary?" If Dean Burgon were living, working, and writing today, would he have been in favor of the revisions of the King James Bible which we have in print today? Would he have been in favor of today's revisions of the Greek Textus Receptus? To both of these important questions, I believe the answer would be a loud, resounding, emphatic, thunderous "No, no, a thousand times no!" The evidence and proof of this response will be seen as this study unfolds.

> **6.**   **Because the New Testament Greek Textus Receptus Has Been Revised by Professor Zane Hodges and Others.** The work of Zane Hodges, formerly of Dallas Theological Seminary, is known to most of those who have studied the Greek textual issues. He and Arthur Farstad, in the 1980's, developed the so-called "Majority Greek Text." The question, however, that comes to my mind, is, "Would Dean Burgon be in favor of the revision of the Textus Receptus at this time and in this manner?" Were they well enough trained in the science of textual criticism? Did they know enough of the languages with which this field deals? Did they have up-to-date indexes of the various sources such as the Church Fathers' quotations of the Scriptures? Many other

questions must be raised along this line. Dean Burgon was very conservative relative to his ideas of when a revision of the Greek New
Testament Textus Receptus could or should take place. He was even more
conservative as to when or even **if** a revision of the English King James
Bible should be undertaken. Dean Burgon had many **WARNINGS** concerning such revisions. Because of his expertise in this field of study, his
WARNINGS should not fall upon deaf ears. They should be listened to
carefully, respected, and then followed.

B.   How Will This Study Be Made? Though Dean John
William Burgon, in his many books, touches on this theme in various
places, this study will concern itself with only one of those works, namely
The Revision Revised. His book was originally three articles reprinted from
the *Quarterly Review*--(1) "The New Greek Text;" (2) "The New English
Version;" and (3) "Westcott and Hort's New Textual Theory." This *Revision Revised* is available either from The Bible For Today or from the
Dean Burgon Society for a gift to either of these groups of **$25.00 + $5.00
S&H.** Ask for **#611**. The Dean Burgon Society reprinted this book in
hardback in 1997. With this book back in print, the reader will be able to
check each quotation from Dean Burgon and to see for himself that I have
quoted accurately and fully at every point of this study.

The Revision Revised had as its major contribution and objective the
consideration of this very question. After the appearance in 1881 of both
the Westcott and Hort Greek textual revision of the Textus Receptus and of
the English Revised Version revision of the time-honored King James
Bible, just exactly what did either or both of them actually accomplish? In
Dean Burgon's mind, was it then time to bring out a Greek textual revision
as they had made at the time? The answer is "No." Was it even then the
time to bring out a Greek textual revision along other lines such as Dean
Burgon himself would espouse? The answer is "No." Was it then the time
to bring out a revision of the King James Bible such as the English Revised
Version (E.R.V.)? The answer is "No." Was it even the time to bring out
a revision of the King James Bible in any form? The answer again is "No."
For proof of this assessment, please continue reading this study carefully.
You will discover why my conclusion is accurate.

Extensive quotation has been made from Dean Burgon's *Revision
Revised* so as to put into his own words his **WARNINGS** and prerequisites for major revision either of the New Testament Greek text or of
the Traditional English text, the Authorized King James Bible.

C.   Organization of the Remainder of the Study.
Section II dealt with Dean Burgon's **WARNINGS** concerning revision of

the Greek text of the Textus Receptus. Section III took up Dean Burgon's **WARNINGS** concerning revision of the English Text to take the place of the King James (Authorized) Bible. Section IV made a number of items in both SUMMARY and in CONCLUSION on this important subject.

II.
DEAN JOHN BURGON'S
WARNINGS CONCERNING
REVISION OF THE
NEW TESTAMENT
GREEK TEXTUS RECEPTUS

A. Dean John Burgon Felt the Textus Receptus Was a Good Text and Better by Far than that of Either Lachmann, Tregelles, Tischendorf, or Westcott and Hort. In this connection, let us examine some of Dean Burgon's quotations in his *Revision Revised* which was written in 1883, and which contains a total of 591 pages. For convenience, for the most part, I will refer to the quotations from Dean Burgon as they occur in page-order in this book, rather than strictly by subject-matter. This will enable the reader to see the subject in depth, and judge for himself concerning the true views of Dean Burgon, whom I consider to have been a master in the field of New Testament textual criticism.

1. Dean Burgon's Criticism of Lachmann's Textual Principles. Dean Burgon wrote:

> Lachman's ruling principle then, was exclusive reliance on a very few ancient authorities--because they are "ancient." He constructed his Text on three or four,--not unfrequently on one or two--Greek codices. Of the Greek Fathers, he relied on Origen. Of the oldest Versions, he cared only for the Latin. To the Syriac (concerning which, see above, p. 9), he paid no attention. We venture to think his method irrational. [Dean Burgon, *Revision Revised*, pp. 242-43]

Lachmann's erroneous principles began in about 1831, and prevailed ever since. Dean Burgon makes it clear that he does not consider any revision of the Textus Receptus based upon but "one or two" or even "three or four" Greek codices, and only one Father and only one Version anything but an "irrational" method. To this I agree completely.

2. Dean Burgon's Criticism of Tregelles' Same

Strange Textual Principles. Dean Burgon wrote

> Tregelles adopted the same strange method. His proceeding is exactly that of a man, who--in order that he may the better explore a comparatively unknown region--begins By putting out both his eyes, and resolutely refuses the help of the natives to show him the way. Why he rejected the testimony of every Father of the IVth century, except Eusebius,--it were unprofitable to enquire. [Dean Burgon, *Revision Revised, op. cit*, p. 243]

Tregelles fell into the same unstable, unacceptable, false textual trap as did his predecessor, Lachmann. Tregelles held sway from about 1857 to about 1872.

3.   Dean Burgon's Criticism of Tischendorf's Slighting of "Eighty-Nine Ninetieths"of the "Extant Witnesses." Dean Burgon wrote:

> Tischendorf, the last and by far the ablest Critic of the three, knew better than to reject "eighty-nine ninetieths" of the extant witnesses. He had recourse to the ingenious expedient of adducing all the available evidence, but adopting just as little of it as he chose: and he chose to adopt those readings only, which are vouched for by the same little band of authorities whose partial testimony had already proved fatal to the decrees of Lachmann and Tregelles. [Dean Burgon, *Revision Revised,*   p. 243.]

Tischendorf, who held sway from about 1865 to 1872, though he "adduced" all the available evidence, he effectively used only the same small handful of authorities as had Lachmann and Tregelles before him. His methods Dean Burgon considered fatal to the arrival at the true text of Scripture.

4.   Dean Burgon's Summary Assessment of the False Schools of Lachmann, Tregelles, and Tischendorf.

Dean Burgon wrote:

> Enough has been said to show--(the only point we are bent on establishing)--that the one distinctive tenet of the three most famous critics since 1831 has been a superstitious reverence for whatever is found in the same little handful of early--but not the earliest,--nor yet of necessity the purest,--documents. Against this arbitrary method of theirs we solemnly, stiffly remonstrate. "Strange," we venture to exclaim, (addressing the living representatives of the school of Lachmann, and Tregelles, and Tischendorf):--"Strange, that you should not perceive that you are the dupes of a fallacy which is even transparent. You talk of

'Antiquity.' But you must know very well that you actually mean something different. You fasten upon three, or perhaps four,--on two, or perhaps three,--on one, or perhaps two,--documents of the IVth or Vth century. But then, confessedly, these are one, two, three, or four specimens only of antiquity,--not 'antiquity' itself. And what if they should even prove to be unfair samples of antiquity? [Dean Burgon, *Revision Revised, op., cit.,* p. 244].

From this quotation, it can be clearly seen that Dean John William Burgon by no means agreed with the basis on which the revisions of the Greek Textus Receptus were made either by Lachmann, by Tregelles, or by Tischendorf. The basis of textual revision must be other than one, two, three, or four documents purportedly representing "antiquity" which in reality were and are unfair samples of antiquity.

5. Dean Burgon's Refutation of Hort's Praise of Lachmann's Greek Text and His Condemnation of the Texts of Erasmus.

Dr. Hort informs us that Lachmann's text of 1831 was "the first founded on documentary authority." . . . on what then, pray, does the learned Professor imagine that the texts of Erasmus (1516) and of Stunica (1522) were founded? His statement is incorrect. The actual difference between Lachmann's text and those of the earlier editors is, that his "documentary authority" is partial, narrow, self-contradictory and is proved to be untrustworthy by a free appeal to antiquity. Their documentary authority, derived from independent sources,--though partial and narrow as that on which Lachmann relied,--exhibits (*under the good Providence of God*) a Traditional Text the general purity of which 350 years of subsequent research have succeeded in accumulating, and which is confessedly the text of A.D. 375. [Dean Burgon, *Revision Revised, op. cit*, p. 250]

In this quotation, Dean Burgon clearly expressed his confidence in the Textus Receptus Greek texts of Erasmus and Stunica, stating that it is of "general purity" and which is "confessedly the text of A.D. 375." This is a strong recommendation for the Textus Receptus--especially in comparison with the text of Lachmann, Tregelles, Tischendorf, or even Westcott and Hort.

6. Dean Burgon's Statements About the Textus Receptus in General and Its Fundamental Soundness and History.

a. Even the Enemy of the Textus Recep-

tus, Hort, Admitted That Its Text Is the "Text of the
Second Half of the Fourth Century."** Dean Burgon wrote
(speaking of Dr. Hort's words in his *INTRODUCTION* to his new Greek
Text of 1881):

> Impatient for argument (at page 92,) we read as follows:--
>> "The fundamental Text of late extant Greek MSS generally
>> is beyond all question identical with the dominant
>> Antiochian or Graeco-Syrian text of the second half of the
>> fourth century."
>
> We request, in passing, that the foregoing statement may be carefully
> noted. The Traditional Greek text of the New Testament,--the
> Textus Receptus, in short is, according to Dr. Hort, "beyond all
> question" the "text of the second half of the fourth century." We
> shall gratefully avail ourselves of his candid admission, by and by.
> [Dean Burgon, *Revision Revised,* pp. 257-258.]

This is a powerful admission on the part of Dr. Hort. Dean Burgon uses it
greatly later in his book to excellent argumentative advantage to further
demolish the house of cards on which the entire Westcott-Hort false theory
has been erected. In other words, the Traditional Greek text or the Textus
Receptus represents antiquity. Dean John William Burgon uses these two
terms as *"in short"* the very same. In fact, it represents antiquity as great
or even greater than that purported to be given to Westcott and Hort's
favorite documents "B" (Vatican) and "Aleph" (Sinai).

**b.   Dean Burgon Praised the "Traditional" or "Re-
ceived" Text as Having the Backing of Antiquity and
Having a Date of From A.D. 350 to A.D. 400.** Dean Burgon
wrote:

> The one great Fact, which especially troubles him and his joint
> Editor, [He is speaking of Hort and Westcott here]--(as well it
> may)--is The Traditional Greek text of the New Testament
> Scriptures. Call this text Erasmian or Complutensian--the text
> of Stephens, or of Beza, or of the Elzevirs,--call it the "received"
> or the Traditional Greek Text or whatever other name you
> please;--the fact remains, that a text has come down to us which
> is attested by a general consensus of ancient copies, ancient
> Fathers, ancient versions. This, at all events, is a point on which,
> (happily,) there exists entIre conformity of opinion between
> Dr. Hort and ourselves. Our readers cannot have yet forgotten
> his virtual admission that,--beyond all question the Textus
> Receptus is the dominant Graeco-Syrian text of A.D. 350 to
> A.D. 400. [Dean Burgon, *Revision Revised,* p. 269.]

Dean Burgon, in his masterful style, used various Greek texts by different names, yet equated them for the most part as being identical. Note these names: (1) the Traditional Text; (2) the Erasmian text; (3) the Complutensian text; (4) the Stephens text; (5) the Beza text; (6) the Elzevir text; (7) the Received Text; and (8) the Textus Receptus. He then agrees wholeheartedly with Westcott and Hort that this eight-named text, that is, the *"Textus Receptus,"* is the dominant text of A.D. 350 to A.D. 400. Note also that Dean Burgon said that this eight-named text is *"attested by a general consensus"* of (1) ancient copies, (2) ancient Fathers, and (3) ancient versions.

c.   Dean Burgon Further Praised the "Traditional" or "Received Text" as Having the Backing of "Every Extant Lectionary of the Greek Church." Dean Burgon wrote:

> In marked contrast to the Text we speak of,--(which is identical with the text of every extant Lectionary of the Greek Church, and may therefore reasonably claim to be spoken of as the Traditional Text.) . . . [Dean Burgon, *Revision Revised,* p. 269.]

This is a fourth ancient documentation favoring the Received text, namely, (4) ancient Greek Lectionaries. These "Lectionaries" are the Scripture portions which were read in the Greek-speaking churches during their church services through the years. Dean Burgon therefore has a fourfold attestation of (1) ancient copies; (2) ancient Fathers, (3) ancient versions, and (4) ancient Greek Lectionaries to bolster and to back up the Textus Receptus or Traditional Text of the New Testament.

d.   Dean Burgon Praised This "Traditional Text" as One Which "Cannot Seriously Be Suspected of Error." Dean Burgon wrote:

> All of these then are with the Traditional Text: which cannot seriously be suspected of error.   [Dean Burgon, *Revision Revised,* p. 356, footnote.]

This is certainly a strong supporting statement by Dean Burgon for the Traditional Received text.

e.   Dean Burgon Believed in Using the "Received Text" as a "Common Standard" of Comparison to Other Greek Texts Since It Was "More Than 1500 Years Old." Dean Burgon wrote:

> We must have some standard whereby to test,--wherewith to compare,--manuscripts. What is more, (give me leave to assure you,) to the end of tIme it wilt probably be the practice of

scholars to compare, mss. Of the New Testament with the "Received Text." The hopeless discrepancies between our five "old uncials," can in no more convenient way be exhibited, than by referring each of them in turn to one and the same common standard. And,--what standard more reasonable and more convenient than the text which, by the good Providence of God, was universally employed throughout Europe for the first 300 years after the invention of printing? being practically identical with the text which (as you yourself admit) was in popular use at the end of three centuries from the date of the sacred autographs themselves: in other words, being more than 1500 years old. (Dean Burgon, *Revision Revised,* p. 386]

Dean Burgon here pointed out his belief in the validity of using the "Received text" or "Textus Receptus" as a standard of comparison which would be used *"to the end of time."* He also said this "Received Text" was "practically identical" to the text which was in existence at the end of *"three centuries"* from the date of the autographs, and which was *"more than 1500 years old."* He also pointed out that the "Received Text" was used for the first 300 years after the *"invention of printing"* throughout all of Europe.

f.   Dean Burgon Scolded Bishop Ellicott for Heaping "Contempt" on the "Humblest Ancestor" of the "Textus Receptus," That Is, "the First Edition of Erasmus." Dean Burgon wrote to Bishop Ellicott, the Chairman of the Committee of the English Revised Version of 1881:

First then, for your strenuous endeavour (pp. 7-10) to prejudice the question by pouring contempt on the humblest ancestor of the Textus Receptus--namely, the first edition of Erasmus. You know very well that the "Textus Receptus" is not the first edition of Erasmus. Why then do you so describe its origin as to imply that it is? You ridicule the circumstances under which a certain ancestor of the family first saw the light. . . . Having in this way done your best to blacken a noble house by dilating on the low ebb to which its fortunes were reduced at a critical period of its history . . . [Dean Burgon, *Revision Revised,* p. 389]

Dean Burgon rightly charged Ellicott with the twisting of his argument against the "Textus Receptus" by equating it with Erasmus's First Edition. To the unlearned readers, this would cause them to draw wrong inferences.

g.   Dean Burgon Reminded Ellicott of His Own Words Concerning the History and Pedigree of the "Received Text" Which Was "Contemporary With   or

"Older Than Any" of the Oldest of Our Extant Manuscript of the Greek New Testament. Dean Burgon wrote (quoting Bishop Ellicott himself directly):

> "The manuscripts which Erasmus used differ for the most part, only in small and insignificant details from the bulk of the cursive manuscripts. The general character of their text is the same. By this observation the pedigree of the Received Text is carried up beyond the individual manuscripts used by Erasmus . . . That pedigree stretches back to a remote antiquity. The first ancestor of the Received Text was at least contemporary with the oldest of our extant manuscripts, if not older than any one of them." [Dean Burgon, *Revision Revised*, pp. 11, 12.]

By your own showing therefore, the Textus Receptus is, "at least," 1550 years old. [Dean Burgon, *Revision Revised,* p. 390]
Make no mistake about it, Dean Burgon did not allow Ellicott to get away with saying that the *"Textus Receptus"* began with *"Erasmus"* like so many opponents of the T.R. today have said in their books. *"That pedigree stretches back to a remote antiquity"* wrote Ellicott. It is important for us today to realize this as well.

h.   Dean Burgon Pointed Out the "Two Distinct Lines of Descent" of the Traditional [Received] Text, Namely The "Complutensian" as Well as the "Erasmian." Dean Burgon wrote:

> And the genealogy of the written, no less than the genealogy of the Incarnate Word, is traceable back by two distinct lines of descent, remember: for the"Complutensian," which was printed in 1514, exhibits the "Traditional Text" with the same general fidelity as the "Erasmian," which did not see the light till two years later. [Dean Burgon, *Revision Revised*, 2p. cit., pp. 390-91]

The Complutensian Polyglot of 1514 was just as much a part of the "Traditional" or "Received" Text of the Greek New Testament as were the editions of Erasmus.

i.   Dean Burgon Esteemed the "Received Text" Which Was in His Time Over "1550 Years Old" and Even "Older," As "Quite Good Enough For All Ordinary Purposes." Dean Burgon wrote:

> For my part, being fully convinced, like yourself, that essentially the Received Text is full 1550 years old,--(yes, and a vast deal

older,)--I esteem it quite good enough for all ordinary purposes.
. . . (Dean Burgon, *Revision Revised*, p. 392.]

Though, as we shall see in a later section of this present study, Dean Burgon had some minor modifications he would make in the Textus Receptus, yet he *"esteemed it"* as being *"quite good enough for all ordinary purposes."*

7.   Dean Burgon Felt Strongly That the "Revision" of the "Textus Receptus" Made in 1881 by Westcott and Hort Was the Worst Sort Imaginable Because of the False Principles and Theories Upon Which That "Revision" Was Founded.   In this discussion of when Dean John William Burgon would make a major revision of the Textus Receptus, it is most appropriate to quote a few of Dean Burgon's words in total opposition to the "major revision" of that Textus Receptus made by the two professors, Westcott and Hort in 1881.   We find that such a "major revision" as was made then (and which has since been received and accepted as a new Received text by multitudes of both liberals, neo-evangelicals, and many "fundamentalists") was, in almost every case, the exact opposite of what Dean Burgon would have suggested.   This was so because it was based upon fallacious principles and an erroneous theory.

a.   Dean Burgon's "One Object" Was to "Defeat" the "Revision of the Sacred Text" of Westcott and Hort Which Is "Untrustworthy From Beginning to End".
Dean Burgon wrote:

My one object has been to defeat the mischievous attempt which was made in 1881 to thrust upon this Church and realm a revision of the Sacred Text, which--recommended though it be by eminent names--I am thoroughly convinced and am able to prove, is untrustworthy from beginning to end. The reason is plain. It has been constructed throughout on an utterly erroneous hypothesis. [Dean Burgon, *Revision Revised,* pp. v-vi.]

This statement is crystal clear as to its meaning and purport.

b.   Dean Burgon Held That Westcott and Hort's Perversion of the Textus Receptus Was a "Poisoning of the River of Life at its Sacred Source."
Dean Burgon wrote:

It is, however, the systematic depravation of the underlying Greek which does so grievously offend me: for this is nothing else but a poisoning of the River of Life at its Sacred source. Our revisers, (with the best and purest intentions, no doubt,) stand convicted of having deliberately rejected the Words of

Inspiration in every page, and of having substituted for them fabricated readings which the Church has long since refused to acknowledge, or else has rejected with abhorrence; and which only survive at this time in a little handful of documents of the most depraved type. [Dean Burgon, *Revision Revised,* pp. vi-vii.]

These are explosive words, yet they are factually true. This is exactly what the Westcott and Hort Greek textual "Fabricators" have done.

c.   **Dean Burgon Charged the Westcott and Hort "Revision" as Causing the "Words of Inspiration" to Be "Seriously Imperilled."** Dean Burgon wrote:

If, therefore any do complain that I have sometimes hit my opponents rather hard, I take leave to point out that "to every thing there is a season, and a time to every purpose under the sun": "a time to embrace, and a time to be far from embracing": a time for speaking smoothly, and a time for speaking sharply. And that when the Words of Inspiration are seriously imperilled, as now they are, it is scarcely possible for one who is determined effectually to preserve the deposit in its integrity, to hit either too straight or too hard. [Dean Burgon, *Revision Revised,* pp. vii-viii.]

What a warrior of the Word was Dean Burgon. What purpose. What determination. Would to God that He would raise up a whole generation of Dean Burgons to rise up like men and be counted in our present-day assault on the Words of God by the current Greek revisions and English perversions. "Is there not a cause?"

d.   **Dean Burgon Branded the Westcott and Hort Textual "Revision" As Being"the Most Depraved Which Has Ever Appeared in Print."** Dean Burgon wrote:

On that Greek Text of theirs [That is, that of Westcott and Hort], (which I hold to be the most depraved which has ever appeared in print), . . . [Dean Burgon, *Revision Revised,* p. xxx.]

This is Dean Burgon's assessment of the Westcott-Hort Greek text. Their claim for their text, however, was that

"it exhibits a closer approximation to the inspired autographs than the world has hitherto seen." [Dean Burgon, *Revision Revised,* p. 2]

This latter statement, however, is patently false, as will be seen from a diligent reading of Dean Burgon's books on the text. The exact opposite is true.

> **e. Dean Burgon Stated That the Westcott and Hort "Revision" Was "Vastly More Remote from the Inspired Autographs" Than Any "Which Has Appeared Since the Invention of Printing."** Dean Burgon wrote:

> With regret we record our conviction, that these accomplished scholars [that is, Westcott and Hort] have succeeded in producing a text vastly more remote from the inspired autographs of the evangelists than any which has appeared since the invention of printing. [Dean Burgon, *Revision Revised,* pp. 25-26.1

> **f. Dean Burgon Stated That "Conjectural Emendation" Such as That Used in the Westcott and Hort "Revision" Has "No Place" in "Biblical Textual Criticism."** Dean Burgon wrote:

> May we be allowed to assure the accomplished writer that in Biblical textual criticism, "conjectural emendation" has no place? [Dean Burgon, *Revision Revised,* p. 28.]

This principle can be applied to the Old Testament text as well as to the New Testament text--even in our own day, when *"conjectural emendation"* is an "acceptable method" on the part of many, including some "fundamentalists."

> **g. Dean Burgon Faulted the Westcott and Hort "Revision" as Being "Palpably Mistaken" for Changing the Textus Receptus at Luke 2:14 and Mark 16:9-20.** Dean Burgon wrote:

> We may not go on doubting for ever. The "angelic hymn" and "the last 12 verses" of S. Mark's Gospel, are convenient places for a trial Of strength. It has now been proved that the commonly received text of S. Luke ii.14 is the true text--the Revisionists' emendation of the place, a palpable mistake. [Dean Burgon, *Revision Revised,* p. 47]

The same could be said for our modern versions in English, where the same errors are present, and are also a *"palpable mistake."*

> **h. Dean Burgon Stated That the Westcott and Hort Text Departed From the Traditional Text "Nearly 6,000 Times" and Almost "Invariably for the Worse."** Dean Burgon wrote:

> . . . the "new Greek text" put forth by the Revisionists of our Authorized Bible is utterly inadmissible. The Traditional Text has been departed from by them nearly 6000 times;--almost

invariably for the worse. [Dean Burgon, *Revision Revised,* p. 107.]

i. Dean Burgon Downed the Westcott and Hort Text as Being "More Remote"From the Originals Than Any to Have Seen the Light. Dean Burgon wrote:

> It has been the ruin of the present undertaking--as far as the Sacred Text is concerned--that the majority of the Revisionist body have been misled throughout by the oracular decrees and impetuous advocacy of Drs. Westcott and Hort; who, with the purest intentions and most laudable industry, have constructed a text demonstrably more remote from the Evangelic verity than any which has ever yet seen the light. [Dean Burgon, *Revision Revised,* p. 110.]

j. Dean Burgon Labeled Westcott and Hort's Text to Be "the Most Vicious Recension of the Original Greek in Existence". Dean Burgon wrote:

> Who could have anticipated that the opportunity would have been adroitly seized to inflict upon the Church the text of Drs. Westcott and Hort, in all its essential features,--a text which, as will be found elsewhere largely explained, we hold to be the most vicious Recension of the original Greek in existence? [Dean Burgon, *Revision Revised,* p. 114.]

More plain language from Dean John Burgon.

k. Dean Burgon Said That the Westcott and Hort "Invented" Text Was "a Thousand Times Worse" Than the "Text" of "Erasmus," the "Complutensian," "Stephens," "Beza," or the "Elzevirs," Because It Is "Hopelessly Depraved Throughout". Dean Burgon wrote:

> For the Greek text which they have invented proves to be so hopelessly depraved throughout, that if it were to be thrust upon the church's acceptance, we should be a thousand times worse off than we were with the text which Erasmus and the Complutensian,--Stephens, and Beza, and the Elzevirs,--bequeathed to us upwards of three centuries ago. [Dean Burgon, *Revision Revised, op. cit.,* p. 118.]

This is a strong indictment of the Westcott and Hort revisionist depravity in favor of the "Textus Receptus." These Textus Receptus editions, according to Dean Burgon, are *"1,000 times"* better than the text of Westcott and Hort. That's quite a superiority, wouldn't you think?

l. Dean Burgon Accused Westcott and Hort's Text of "Falsifying the Inspired Greek Text in

Countless Places" and at the Same Time "Branding with Suspicion" Some Of The "Most Precious Utterances of the Spirit." Dean Burgon wrote:

> Shame,--yes, shame on that two-thirds majority of well-intentioned but most incompetent men, who,--finding themselves (in an evil hour) appointed to correct "plain and clear errors" in the English "Authorized Version,"--occupied themselves instead with falsifying the insp I red Greek text in countless places., and branding with suspicion some of the most precious utterances of the Spirit. Shame--yes, shame upon them. [Dean Burgon, *Revision Revised*, p. 135]

There was therefore a double fault with the Westcott and Hort Greek text. It put false words into Scripture that never should be there, and then at the same time, branded with suspicion many of the genuine words of the Holy Spirit! As Jeremiah wrote:

> *"For my people have committed two evils; they have forsaken me the fountain of living waters, and hewed them out cisterns, broken cisterns, that can hold no water"* (Jeremiah 2:13).

m.   Dean Burgon Assailed Westcott and Hort's Erection of the "Two IVth-Century Copies" Into an "Authority from Which There Shall Be No Appeal." Dean Burgon wrote:

> As for the weak superstition of these last days, which--without proof of any kind--would erect two IVth-century copies of the New Testament [i.e. "B" and "Aleph"], (demonstrably derived from one and the same utterly depraved archetype,) into an authority from which there shall be no appeal,--it cannot be too soon or too unconditionally abandoned. [Dean Burgon, *Revision Revised*, pp. 227-28.]

Oh that our present-day fundamentalists and neo-evangelicals (and the liberals as well) might agree with this important point by Dean Burgon. The present-day modern translations of the New Testament, for the most part and without many exceptions, are following slavishly these same two corrupt documents that Westcott and Hort followed in 1881, namely, the Vatican ("B") and the Sinai ("Aleph") manuscripts.

n.   Dean Burgon Labeled the Westcott and Hort "Revision" as a "Prodigious Blunder" Containing "Vile Fabrications" From Which God Preserved "Erasmus and Stunica,--Stephens and Beza and the Elzevirs." Dean Burgon Wrote:

> It is already admitted on all hands that the Revision has been a

prodigious blunder. How it came about that, with such a first-rate textual critic among them as Prebendary Scrivener, the Revisers of 1881 should have deliberately gone back to those vile fabrications from which the good Providence of God preserved Erasmus and Stunica--Stephens and Beza and the Elzevirs--three centuries ago; . . . [Dean Burgon, *Revision Revised,* pp. 237-38.]

This quote would point out Dean Burgon's strong preference, without any question whatsoever, for the "Textus Receptus" of Erasmus, Stunica, Stephens, Beza and the Elzivers as over against the Westcott and Hort "revised Greek text."

o.   Dean Burgon Decried the "Embalming" of "Their Errors" Rather Than Rejecting Them as Found In "B," "ALEPH," the "Coptic Version," "D," and the "Old Latin Copies." Dean Burgon wrote:

In marked contrast to the text we speak of,--(which is identical with the text of every extant Lectionary of the Greek Church, and may therefore reasonably claim to be spoken of as the Traditional Text,)--is that contained in a little handful of documents of which the most famous are codices B, Aleph, and the Coptic version (as far as it is known), on the one hand,--cod. D and the Old Latin copies , on the other. To magnify the merits of these as helps and guides, and to ignore their many patent and scandalous defects and blemishes:--*per fas et nefas* to vindicate their paramount authority wherever it is in any way possible to do so; and when that is clearly impossible, then to treat their errors as the ancient Egyptians treated the I r cats, dogs, monkeys, and other vermin,--namely to embalm them, and pay them divine honours:--such for the last 50 years has been the practice of the dominant school of textual criticism among ourselves. [Dean Burgon, *Revision Revised,* pp. 269-70.]

Again, Dean Burgon rebukes the *"embalming"* of *"many patent and scandalous defects and blemishes"* such as Westcott and Hort (as well as their present-day followers) have done.

p.   Dean Burgon Lamented Westcott and Hort's "Ruthlessly Sacrificing" the Great Majority of "Copies, Fathers, & Versions" on the "Altar" of "the Oracle." The *"oracle"* is, "codex B." Dean Burgon wrote:

Behold then the altar at which copies, Fathers are all to be ruthlessly sacrificed:--the tribunal from which there shall be absolutely no appeal:--the oracle, which is to silence every

doubt, resolve every riddle, smooth away every difficulty. All
has been stated, where the name has been pronounced of--
codex B. [Dean Burgon, *Revision Revised,* p. 301.]
Certainly, this methodology must not be acceptable today any more than it
was in Dean Burgon's day. Yet this is the very method, for the most part,
used by the N.E.V., the N.A.S.V., the A.S.V., the R.S.V., the N.I.V., the
L.V., the T.E.V., and the others (with the exception of the K.J.B.). Even the
N.K.J.V. study edition in the footnotes, gives these alternative textual
readings as possibilities.

> **q.   Dean Burgon Characterized "Codices B
and Aleph" as "Impure," "Two of the Least Trustworthy
Documents in Existence," "the Foulest Text that Had
Ever Seen the Light," and "Specimens of the Depraved
Class."** Dean Burgon wrote:

> (I) the impurity of the texts exhibited by codices B and Aleph
> is not a matter of opinion, but a matter of fact.' These are two
> of the least trustworthy documents in existence . . . . "a text
> formed" by "taking codex B as the sole authority" "would be"
> . . . by far the foulest text that had ever seen the light: worse.,
> that is to say, even than the text of Drs. Westcott and Hort. .
> . . and codices B and Aleph are nothing else but specimens
> demonstrably of the depraved class thus characterized. [Dean
> Burgon, *Revision Revised,* pp. 315-317.]

Dean Burgon has been saying similar things many times as we have quoted
above, but we wish to be complete, and not leave out very many of his
choice words of condemnation on the entire Westcott and Hort "house of
cards" which must by God's grace come crashing down once and for all in
this 20th and 21st century of ours.

> **r.   Dean Burgon Denounced the Major
Documents Underlying the Westcott and Hort "Revision
of the Greek Text" ("B," "Aleph," & "C") With Specific
Defects Enumerated.** Dean Burgon wrote:

> As for codex Aleph, it carries on its face its own effectual
> condemnation~aptly illustrating the precept *fiat experimentum
> in corpore vili.* It exhibits the efforts of many generations of
> men to restore its text,--(which, as proceeding from the first
> scribe," is admitted by one of its chief admirers to be "very
> rough")--to something like purity. "At least ten different
> revisers," from the IVth to the XIIth century, are found to have
> tried their hands upon it."--codex C, after having had "at least
> three correctors very busily at work upon it." (in the VIth and

IXth centuries), finally (in the xiith) was fairly obliterated--
literally scraped out,--to make room for the writings of a Syrian
father.--I am therefore led by a priori considerations to augur ill
of the contents of B, Aleph, C. [Dean Burgon, *Revision Revised,*
p. 325.]

It is strange, indeed, in view of such *"condemnation"* from the face of
"Aleph" and"C" themselves to their having been tampered with, that
modern-day fundamentalist leaders (and followers, for that matter, as well)
cannot break clean with the Westcott and Hort group of texts (such as "B,"
"Aleph, & "C"). and have nothing whatever to do with their products of
translation, such as the NEV. NIV, NASV, ASV, RSV, LV, TEV, and
many, many others.

**s.   Dean Burgon Denominated as "Ridicu-
lous," "More than Unreasonable," "Weak Superstition,"
"Craven Homage and "Simply Worthless" the Westcott
and Hort Prize Manuscripts, "B," "Aleph," and "C."** Dean
Burgon wrote:

But when I find them [that is, "B," "Aleph," and "C"] hopelessly
at variance among themselves: above all, when I find (1) all other manuscripts of whatever date,--(2) the most ancient versions,--and (3) the whole body of the primitive Fathers, decided-
ly opposed to them--I am (to speak plainly) at a loss to understand how any man of sound understanding acquainted with
all the facts of the case and accustomed to exact reasoning, can
hesitate to regard the unsupported (or the slenderly supported)
testimony of one or other of them as simply worthless. The
craven homage which the foremost of the three [that is,"B,"]
habitually receives at the hands of Drs. Westcott and Hort, I
can only describe as a weak superstition. It is something more
than unreasonable. It becomes even ridiculous. [Dean Burgon,
Revision Revised, p. 325.]

Certainly Dean Burgon would not advocate building any "revision" of the
"Textus Receptus"on anything similar to or like the principles on which
Westcott and Hort built their "revision." Quite the contrary.

**t.   Dean Burgon Acknowledged Both the
"General Trustworthiness" of the "Traditional [Re-
ceived] Text," and the "Essential Rottenness" of the
"Greek Text" of Westcott and Hort**. Dean Burgon wrote:

And yet, it was no isolated place which I was eager to establish,
when at first I took up my pen. It was the general trustworthiness of the Traditional Text,--(the text which you admit to be

upwards of 1500 years old,)--which I aimed at illustrating: the essential rottenness of the foundation on which the Greek text of the revision of 1881 has been constructed by yourself and your fellow revisers,--which I was determined to expose. [Dean Burgon, *Revision Revised,* p. 516.]

Dean Burgon, in writing to Bishop Ellicott, the Chairman of the Revision Committee of 1881 on which Drs. Hort and Westcott sat, summed up his belief in the vast superiority of the "Traditional Text" as over against the inferior "Westcott and Hort" "revision" of that text in 1881. It is interesting to note that the vast majority of modern translations of the New Testament from Greek to English have as their foundation this very same fallacious text that Dean Burgon exposed in his *Revision Revised* of 1883. Over 100 years have transpired since its publication, and the ill-informed, the ill-advised, and the ill-prepared "scholars" of today are still reverencing (almost to the point of worship) virtually the same Greek text that this giant of textual critics called by all the "choice" names which have been quoted up to this point. When will we learn from history so that we do not have to repeat that same history?

B.   Dean John Burgon Felt That, Though the Textus Receptus Was an Excellent Text For the Use in the Meantime, and Was a "Thousand Times" Superior to the Greek Text of Westcott and Hort, Yet He Did Not Hold to its "Perfection."   I do not want anyone reading this to misunderstand Dean John William Burgon's position on the "Textus Receptus" or the "Traditional Text." Dean Burgon held it to be superior to the text of Westcott and Hort or any of that school of false textual critics. He did feel, however, that it was not "perfect." If revised, it should be properly revised in the minor places where it might need such. Any such revision must adhere strictly upon the principles laid down by this master textual critic. Until then, the Textus Receptus was to be used without apology as the printed text closest to the original autographs of any in print today.

1.   Dean Burgon Used the "Commonly Received Text" as a "Common Standard," Not as "the Final Standard of Appeal."   Dean Burgon wrote:

I have referred five famous codices (A B ℵ C D)--certain of which are found to have turned the brain of critics of the new school--to one and the same familiar exhibition of the commonly received text of the New Testament: but by so doing I have not by any means assumed the textual purity of that common

standard. In other words, I have not made it "the final standard
of appeal." all critics, wherever found,--at all times, have collated
with the commonly Received Text: but only as the most
convenient standard of comparison not, surely as the absolute
standard of excellence. [Dean Burgon, *Revision Revised,* pp.
xviii-xix.]

This is an honest statement of Dean Burgon's view of the "Textus Receptus"
or "Received Text." he did not think it was perfect, but needed minor
improvements in spots, but any revision was to be preceded by certain
safeguards of which we'll speak later in this study.

**2.   Dean Burgon Felt the "Textus Receptus"
Does "Call for Revision" But That Must Be Based Upon
"Entirely Different Principles" From Those of Westcott
and Hort's Text.** Dean Burgon wrote:

But (what is a far more important circumstance) we are further
convinced that a prior act of penance to be submitted to by the
revisers would be the restoration of the underlying Greek text
to very nearly--not quite--the state in which they found it when
they entered upon their ill-advised undertaking. "Very nearly--
not quite:--for, in not a few particulars, the "Textus Receptus"
does call for revision, certainly although revision on entirely
different principles from those which are found to have prevailed in the Jerusalem Chamber. [the location of Westcott and
Hort's English Revised Version revision of Greek & English in
1881]. [Dean Burgon, *Revision Revised,* p. 107.]

Though Dean Burgon agreed that the "Textus Receptus" did *"call for
revision,"* he said the *"principles"* on which such revision should be based
were diametrically opposite to those used by Westcott and Hort in their
revised Greek text which was used as the basis for the English Revised
Version of 1881 (E.R.V.). He further stated that it was his firm belief that
the *"revisers"* should do *"penance"* by *"restoring"* the *"underlying Greek
text to very nearly--not quite--the state in which they found it when they entered upon their ill-advised undertaking."* In part, such a "restoration" has
been made possible by the Trinitarian Bible Society in 1976, by their
printing of the New Testament--the Greek text underlying the English
Authorized Bible of 1611. It is available from the Bible For Today for a
gift of **$14.00, B.F.T. #471**]. This is a reproduction of the text of Dr.
Frederick H. A. Scrivener which gives the exact Greek text underlying the
King James Bible. This is a very readable and scholarly work which every
pastor, and every Christian worker and every layman should have in their
library.

3.   Dean Burgon Felt the "Textus Receptus" Needed "Revision" in "Many of its Lesser Details," But That It Was "an Excellent Text as it Stands" That Will "Never Lead Critical Students of Scripture Seriously Astray." Dean Burgon wrote:

> Obtained from a variety of sources [that is, the Textus Receptus or the Traditional Greek Text] this text proves to be essentially the same in all. That it requires revision in respect of many of its lesser details is undeniable: but it is at least as <u>certain that it is an excellent text as it stands, and that the use of it will never lead critical students of Scripture seriously astray</u>,--which is what no one will venture to predicate concerning any single critical edition of the N.T. which has been published since the days of Griesbach, by the disciples of Griesbach's school. [Dean Burgon, *Revision Revised,* p. 269.]

What Dean Burgon is saying very clearly here, is that if he had a choice between using the Textus Receptus or the Traditional Text in its present state, and of using *"any single critical"* Greek text which has been published since the days of Griesbach. It must be remembered that John James Griesbach was a pupil of Semler, who died in 1812, [cf. *Guide to the Textual Criticism of the New Testament* by Edward Miller, pp. 17-18, available as **B.F.T. #743** for a gift of **$7.00 + S&H**]. This would therefore urge our present students in the colleges, Bible institutes, and seminaries of our world to forsake their "critical editions" of the Greek New Testament such as those of (1) Nestle/Aland; (2) Souter; (3) United Bible Society; (4) Westcott and Hort; or any other Griesbachian monstrosity. Dean Burgon was for a return to "square one" in the Greek New Testament for starters. Revision would come later, but for now, he would return to the Textus Receptus.

4.   Dean Burgon Did Not Take the "Received" or Any Other "Text" as a "Standard from Which There Shall Be no Appeal." Dean Burgon wrote:

> But pray--, who in his senses,--what-sane man in Great Britain-- ever dreamed of regarding the "received,"--aye, or any other known "text"--as a "standard from which there shall be no appeal"? Have I ever done so? Have I ever implied as much? If I have, show me where. [Dean Burgon, *Revision Revised,* p. 385.]

What Dean Burgon was saying here is that the state of the Greek New Testament text was such even at his time in 1883, that there was no 100%

certain text in each and every detail *"from which there was to be no appeal"* whatsoever. It would be less than honest for Dean Burgon to have stated that. And yet fundamentalists and neo-evangelicals and liberal-modernists right and left are holding up the critical texts of Westcott and Hort and their colleagues and saying to us, "here it is." There is no appeal from it. This is not correct, said Dean Burgon. Even the Textus Receptus might yield to evidence from Fathers, copies, versions, and Lectionaries **if and only if** certain Burgonian safeguards were to be insured. We shall speak about these "safeguards" later in this study. For my part, everything considered, **we should leave alone the Textus Receptus that underlies the King James Bible**.

> **5.   Dean Burgon Held That the "Received Text" Even in His Day Was "Full 1550 Years Old" and Even "a Vast Deal Older," and He Esteemed It "Quite Good Enough for All Ordinary Purposes, Yet He Sometimes Made "Appeal From It."** Dean Burgon wrote:

> For my own part, being fully convinced, like yourself, [writing to Bishop Ellicott, the Chairman of the English Revised Version Committee of 1881], that essentially the received text is full 1550 years old,--(yes, and a vast deal older)--I esteem it quite good enough for all ordinary purposes. And yet, so far am I from pinning my faith to it, that I eagerly make my appeal from it to the threefold witness of copies, versions, Fathers whenever I find its testimony challenged--   [Dean Burgon, *Revision Revised*, p. 392.]

Again, this is Dean Burgon's solid faith in the essential soundness of the Received Text, and yet his recognition that in *"lesser details,"* the copies, versions, and Fathers might yield slight corrections if properly and soundly used. The *"copies, versions and Fathers"* have not been properly used either in the Greek texts of (1) Westcott and Hort; (2) Nestle-Aland; (3) the United Bible Society: (4) the so-called "MajorityTexts" either of Hodges and Farstad or of Robinson and Peirpont; or (5) any others before or after Dean Buron's time. In other words, no one has done it in the proper method specified in detail by Dean Burgon!

> **C.   Dean John Burgon Felt Strongly As to the Vital Importance of the Church Fathers' Quotations of the New Testament for Critical Use in Revising the Textus Receptus.**

> **1.   Dean Burgon's Knowledge of the Church Fathers' Quotation of the New Testament was Far Superior to That of Both "TISCHENDORF" and "TREGEL-**

LES on Luke 2:14. Dean Burgon wrote, of his study on Luke 2:14, "the angelic hymn" so-called:

> Of the ninety two places above quoted, Tischendorf knew of only eleven, Tregelles adduces only six.--neither critic seems to have been aware that "Gregory Thaum." is not the author of the citation they ascribe to him. And why does Tischendorf quote as Basil's what is known not to have been his? [Dean Burgon, *Revision Revised,* p. 45.]

The masterful knowledge and use of the Church Fathers' original quotations of Luke 2:14 by Dean Burgon to establish once and for all the veracity of the Textus Receptus at this point [cf. pp. 41-47], is mind-boggling, indeed. Whereas Tischendorf knew of only eleven places where the church fathers quoted Luke 2:14, and whereas Tregelles knew only of six places, Dean John William Burgon, the master in the area of Church Fathers' quotations of the Greek New Testament, adduced no less than ninety-five places where Luke 2:14 was quoted by these Church Fathers. Because of the early date of many of these Church Fathers who were known men in history, their testimony often pre-dates by many years or centuries the testimony of either the manuscripts, or the versions, or the Lectionaries.

2.   Dean Burgon Argued in Favor of Use of "Patristic Testimony as Opposed to Hort's Wanting to Get Rid of It. Dean Burgon wrote:

> Does not the learned Professor [that is, Hort] see that, by thus getting rid of the testimony of the whole body of the Fathers he leaves the science which he is so good as to patronize in a most destitute condition,--besides placing himself in a most inconvenient state of isolation? If clear and consentient Patristic testimony to the text of Scripture is not to be deemed forcible witness to its truth,--whither shall a man betake himself for constraining evidence? [Dean Burgon, *Revision Revised,* p. 291

3.   Dean Burgon Explained the Value of Proper Use of Church Fathers Because They were, in Reality, "Dated Codices" as Often as They Bear "Clear Witness to the Text of Scripture." Dean Burgon wrote:

> But then, these men lived within a very few hundred years of the apostles of the Lord Jesus Christ [that is, the Church Fathers did]: and when they witness to the reading of their own copies, their testimony on the point, to say the least, is worthy of our most respectful attention. Dated codices, in fact are they, to all intents and purposes, as often as they bear clear witness to the text of Scripture--a fact, (we take leave to throw out the

remark in passing,) which has not yet nearly attracted the
degree of attention which it deserves. [Dean Burgon, *Revision
Revised,* p. 292]

The previous two quotations show conclusively that Dean Burgon valued
highly the quotations of the Church Fathers when they bore witness to the
very text of the Greek New Testament which that particular Father held in
his hand when he was quoting or alluding to Scripture. He pointed out as
well that the Patristic evidence has not by any means attracted *"the degree
of attention which it deserves."* This is still very much true to the shame of
so-called "Textual Critics" of today.

**4.   Dean Burgon Held That "Every Attesting
Father" Is Not Only a "Dated Manuscript,"But Also "an
Independent Authority."** Dean Burgon wrote:

Upset the hypothesis [the false hypothesis of Westcott and Hort]
on the other hand, and all is reversed in a moment. Every attesting Father is perceived to be a dated MS. and an independent authority; and the combined evidence of several of
these becomes simply unmanageable. [Dean Burgon, *Revision
Revised,* p. 297.]

This is similar to the previous point made by Dean Burgon. Each Father is
"an independent authority" witnessing to the very copy of the Greek New
Testament text he was holding in his hand, or which was resting on his
writing desk from which he quoted or alluded to many, many New
Testament verses.

**5.   Dean Burgon Showed Specifically in What
Ways the False Westcott and Hort Theories Disagreed
With His Stand on the Value of the "Fathers of the
Church."** Dean Burgon wrote:

We comment, in passing, the foregoing dictum of these
accomplished Editors to the critical judgment of all candid and
intelligent Readers. Not as dated manuscripts, therefore, at
least equal in antiquity to the oldest which we now possess;--
not as the authentic utterances of famous doctors and Fathers
of the church (instead of being the work of unknown and
irresponsible scribes):--not as sure witnesses of what was
accounted Scripture in a known region by a famous personage,
at a well-ascertained 'period ' (instead of coming to us, as our
codices universally do, without a history and without a
character):--in no such light are we henceforth to regard
Patristic citations of Scripture:--but only [according to the false
Westcott and Hort theories] "as so many secondary MSS.,

inferior to the better sort of secondary uncials now existing."
That the testimony of the Fathers in the lump, must perforce in
some such way either be ignored or else flouted if the text of
Drs. Westcott and Hort is to stand,--we were perfectly well
aware. It is simply fatal to them: and they know it. [Dean
Burgon, *Revision Revised,* 'p . 299.]

Dean Burgon certainly showed himself, by the preceding words (and many
others as well found throughout *Revision Revised* and his other works) to
be thoroughly convinced of the value of the Church Fathers where they
have quoted or alluded to "Scripture." It is a pity that more present-day
textual critics do not share (as I do very definitely) with Dean Burgon this
sound conviction. There will never be faithful work done in the restoration
of the Traditional Text in the minor details where it needs to be done in the
absence of a thorough-going examination and analysis of Church Fathers'
quotations of and or allusions to the Bible.

**D.   Dean John Burgon Gave Specific Suggestions
as to Both "How" and "When" He Would Make a Major
Revision of the Textus Receptus.** In this section, which is the
most important section in this present division of the study, I will give
quotations from Dean John Burgon's *Revision Revised* that pertain to this
point in the page order as they appear in the book. At the end of this paper,
I shall summarize Dean Burgon's major prerequisites so that they might
stand out clearly for all to see.

**1.   Dean Burgon Believed As an "Indispensable
Condition" of Success in "Textual Criticism" That a Man
"for Many Years Past" Has Given "the Whole of His
Time" and Has "Freely Sacrificed Health, Ease, Relaxation, Even Necessary Rest."** Dean Burgon wrote:

. . . the indispensable condition of success in this department is,
that a man should give to the subject, (which is a very intricate
one and abounds in unexpected problems), his undivided attention for an extended period. I trust there is nothing unreasonable in the suggestion that one who has not done this, should be
very circumspect when he sits in judgment on a neighbour of his
who, for very many years past, has given to textual criticism the
whole of his time;--has freely sacrificed health, ease, relaxation,
even necessary rest to this one object,--has made it his one
business to acquire such an independent mastery of the subject
as shall qualify him to do battle successfully for the imperilled
letter of God's Word. [Dean Burgon, *Revision Revised,* p.
xvii.]

These "indispensable conditions" of Dean Burgon include (1) full time; (2) over a long period of time; (3) with sacrifice of health, ease, relaxation, and necessary rest; (4) with but one object. Where are the men today who qualify in all of these areas? I say confidently, there are none.

2. Dean Burgon Insisted on the "Scientific Method Being Used, Not Westcott and Hort's "Unscientific Method," for Textual Criticism Work Entailing Many "Long Summer Days" With Very Little "to Show" for All the Time Spent. Dean Burgon wrote:

> I know but too well how laborious is the scientific method which I advocate. A long summer day disappears, while the student--with all his appliances about him--is resolutely threshing out some minute textual problem. Another, and yet another bright day vanishes. Comes Saturday evening at last, and a page of illegible manuscript is all that he has to show for a week's heavy toil. *Quosque tandem?* And yet, it is the indispensable condition of progress in an unexplored region, that a few should thus labour until a path has been cut through the forest--a road laid down,--huts built,--a *modus vivendi* established. [Dean Burgon, *Revision Revised,* p. xxv.]

Here, Dean Burgon talks about: (1) something laborious; (2) a scientific method; (3) resolutely threshing out some minute textual problem; (4) a long summer day which disappears; (5) labour; (6) a week's heavy toil; (7) only one page to show for a week's heavy toil; and (8) an indispensable condition of progress. Where are the men today who qualify for all these conditions? I say confidently, there are none.

3. Dean Burgon Held to a "Method" on a "Supposed Doubtful Reading" Which Involved the "Combined Verdict" of "Manuscripts, Versions," and "Fathers" as "Decisive. Dean Burgon wrote:

> The method I persistently advocate in every case of a supposed doubtful reading (I say it for the last time, and request that I may be no more misrepresented,) is, that an appeal shall be unreservedly made to catholic antiquity and that the combined verdict of manuscripts, versions, Fathers, shall be regarded as decisive. [Dean Burgon, *Revision Revised,* p. xxvii.]

This "method" is directly opposite of that "unscientific method" advocated by Westcott and Hort and their followers today. Dean Burgon would not give up his "appeal" which should be *"unreservedly made to catholic antiquity"* including *"manuscripts, versions, Fathers."* What "revisers" of the "Textus Receptus" today, such as professor Zane Hodges, then of Dallas

Theological Seminary, and his helpers, have fulfilled completely this "method"? I do not believe that he did. The same could be said for Dr. Bruce Metzger and others on the committee who have worked on the Nestle/Aland or United Bible Societies' Greek New Testament.

4.   Dean Burgon Considered That a "Carefully Considered Revision" of the "Received Text" Would Only be Possible "After Many Years" After "Gradual Accessions" of Certain Knowledge" In The Field. Dean Burgon wrote:

> Students of the Greek Testament were sure to have their attention called to the subject [that is, Textual Criticism and related topics],--which must always be in the highest degree desirable; and it was to be expected that in this as in every other department of learning, the progress of inquiry would result in gradual accessions of certain knowledge. **After many years** it might be found practicable to put forth by authority a carefully considered revision of the commonly Received Greek text. [Dean Burgon, *Revision Revised,* p. xxix.]

Since virtually ALL of the successors of Dean Burgon have failed to follow his method in textual criticism, these *"gradual accessions"* of *"certain knowledge"* (as were made by Dean Burgon himself, for example), have not been forthcoming. In fact, the Westcott and Hort mentality has taken over in this field, and the result is heavy obfuscation of *"certain knowledge"* and direct contradiction of the same. Hence, we are no closer now than we were in Dean Burgon's day to the *"after many years"* and such a *"carefully considered revision"* of the Received Greek text. **Do it Dean Burgon's way, or leave it alone.**

5.   Dean Burgon's Basis For Any Revision of the Textus Receptus Was a Careful Scrutiny of "Copies," "Versions," "Fathers," and "Lectionaries." Dean Burgon wrote:

> The provision, then, which the Divine Author of Scripture is found to have made for the preservation in its integrity of his written Word, is of a peculiarly varied and highly complex description. First,--by causing that a vast multiplication of copies should be required all down the ages,--beginning at the earliest period, and continuing in an ever-increasing ratio until the actual invention of printing,--He provided the most effective security imaginable against fraud . . . next versions. The necessity of translating the Scriptures into divers languages for the use of different branches of the early church, procured that many an

authentic record has been preserved of the New Testament as it existed in the first few centuries of the Christian era. . . . lastly, the requirements of assailants and apologists alike, the business of commentators, the needs of controversialists and teachers in every age, have resulted in a vast accumulation of additional evidence of which it is scarcely possible to over estimate the importance. For in this way it has come to pass that every famous doctor of the church in turn has quoted more or less largely from the sacred writings and thus has borne testimony to the contents of the codices with which he was individually familiar. . . . in truth, the security which the text of the New Testament enjoys is altogether unique and extraordinary. To specify one single consideration, which has never yet attracted nearly the amount of attention it deserves,-- "Lectionaries" abound, which establish the text which has been publicly read in the churches of the East, from at least A.D. 400 until the time of the invention of printing. [Dean Burgon, *Revision Revised,* pp.8-9, 11.]

In this quotation, Dean Burgon focuses in upon the fourfold basis on which any true or accurate, thorough-going and major revision of the Textus Receptus should take place, (if ever), namely, the judicious and complete use of (1) **all** copies; (2) **all** versions; (3) **all** Church Fathers; and (4) **all** Lectionaries. All of these four things, for Dean Burgon, (and for me and others of the Dean Burgon Society as well) comprise the irreducible minimum, or the *sine qua non* of evidence on which any and all changes (if any) should be tested before being accepted and acceptable. To omit the **full** evidence in any of these four areas, would constitute an abbreviation of the evidence and thus cause the attempt to fail.

The **full** basis which, for example, Professor Zane Hodges, and his co-workers, have used to arrive at his revision of the Textus Receptus, known as the "Majority Greek text," has not been done in this manner at all. Since Zane Hodges and Arthur Farstad did not completely and thoroughly investigate **all** four items above (since they eliminated several of the four) their results are still very tentative and tenuous. Should any reader question this, he or she is invited to examine closely the introductory words of the Hodges/Farstad Greek Text. They should not be accepted as having arrived at the very Words of God Himself in the original in every detail. **Dean Burgon's method in such revision must be followed thoroughly and completely, or the Textus Receptus underlying the King James Bible should be left alone**.

6.   Dean Burgon Stressed "External Evidence"

as the "Only Safe Guide" and Our "Best" Guide to Any Revision of the Textus Receptus, Saying That "Every Part of That "External Evidence" Must Be Examined Carefully. Dean Burgon wrote:

> For we resolutely maintain I that external evidence must after all be our best, our only safe guide and (to come to the point) we refuse to throw in our lot with those who, disregarding the witness of every other known codex--every other version--every other available ecclesiastical writer--insist on following the dictates of a little group of authorities, of which nothing whatever is known with so much certainty as that often, when they concur exclusively, it is to mislead. We speak of codices B or Aleph or D; the IXth-century codex L, and such cursives as 13 or 33; a few copies of the Old Latin and one of the Egyptian versions: perhaps Origen.-- . . . [Dean Burgon, *Revision Revised,* p. 19.]

Dean Burgon, by this quotation, was arguing against the false methods used by Westcott and Hort and their followers who spurn *"external evidence"* almost in its entirety, and use, rather such spurious techniques as "method of genealogy" the "transcriptional probability," the "instinctive processes of criticism," or some other such means. [Cf. Dean Burgon, *Revision Resived*, p. 20.]

7. Dean Burgon Cautions Against Those Who Would "Reject" the "Commonly Received Text" Without Having the "Evidence" From "All" Sources Clearly Understood. Dean Burgon wrote:

> We deem it even axiomatic, that, in every case of doubt or difficulty--supposed or real--our critical method must be the same: namely, after patiently collecting all the available evidence, then, without partiality or prejudice, to adjudicate between the conflicting authorities and loyally to accept that verdict for which there is clearly the preponderating evidence. The best supported reading, in other words, must always be held to be the true reading: and **nothing may be rejected from the commonly Received Text, except on evidence which shall clearly outweigh the evidence for retaining it**.
> [Dean Burgon, *Revision Revised,* p. 20.]

Note Dean Burgon's caution about *"patiently collecting all the available evidence."* If such has not been done, we are not in any condition for any major revision of the *"Received Text."* yet Westcott and Hort, and their followers, have rejected many words from the *"Received Text"* contrary to all of the *"available evidence."* Such examples could be cited as John 7:53--8:11; Mark 16:9-20; 1 Timothy 3:16, and many others.

8.   Dean Burgon Favored the Holding to and to "Letting Alone" the Received Text Whenever "the Evidence" Is About "Evenly Balanced" Because That "Text" Rests On Infinitely Better Manuscript Evidence" Than "Any Ancient Work." Dean Burgon wrote:

> Whenever the evidence is about evenly balanced, few it is hoped will deny that the text which has been "in possession" for three centuries and a half and which rests on infinitely better manuscript evidence than that of any ancient work which can be named--<u>should for every reason be let alone</u>. [Dean Burgon, *Revision Revised,* p. 21.]

In other words, when the evidence is about *"evenly balanced,"* the "Textus Receptus"should be *"let alone"* and let stand unchanged. The reason for it, as explained by Dean Burgon is that this text *"rests on infinitely better manuscript evidence than that of any ancient work which can be named."* This is saying a lot for the "Textus Receptus" and its pedigree

9.   Dean Burgon Cautioned That the Would-Be Textual Critic Should "Begrudge No Amount of Labour" Even to Ascertain "the truth" About "One Single Controverted Word of Scripture." Dean Burgon wrote:

> But then we make it our fundamental rule to reason always from grounds of external evidence--never from postulates of the imagination. Moreover, in the application of our rule, we begrudge no amount of labour: reckoning a long summer's day well spent if it has enabled us to ascertain the truth concerning one single controverted Word of Scripture. [Dean Burgon, *Revision Revised,* p. 96]

Note the *"labour"* that Dean Burgon was very willing to expend even for the determination of but one Word of Scripture which was in question by its critics.

10. Dean Burgon Analyzed the "Exactly Eight" of the "English Revision" Committee Who Would Have Been Capable of Making a Major Revision of the "Textus Receptus" if Specific Requisites Were Insured.   Dean Burgon wrote the following, and I have placed in [brackets] the various numbers of the prerequisites laid out by Dean Burgon in this context:

> Having regard to the Greek text exclusively we also (strange to relate) had singled out exactly eight from the members of the New Testament company--**[I]** divines of undoubted orthodoxy

who for their **[2]** splendid scholarship and **[3]** proficiency in the best learning **[4]** might (as we humbly think), **[5]** under certain safeguards have been **[6]** safely entrusted even with the responsibility of revising the Sacred Text. **[7]** under the guidance of Prebendary Scrivener (who among living Englishmen is *facile princeps* in these pursuits) it is scarcely to be anticipated that, **[8]** when unanimous such divines **[9]** would ever have materially erred. But then, of course, **[10]** a previous **[11]** life-long familiarity with the science of textual criticism **[12]** or at least leisure for prosecuting it now, for ten or twenty years **[13]** with absolutely undivided attention,--would be the indispensable requisite for the success of such an undertaking **[14]** and this, undeniably, is a qualification rather to be desiderated [that is, "desired"] than looked for at the hands of English divines of note in our present day. [Dean Burgon, *Revision Revised,* pp. 108-9.]

Here is perhaps the most clear list of **14 qualifications** or **WARNINGS** about any attempt to revise the "Textus Receptus" in major fashion that we have met with thus far. Note, these include: (1) undoubted orthodoxy on the part of all the revisers; (2) splendid scholarship; (3) proficiency in the best learning; (4) and even then it is *"might"* or a tentative guess; (5) only under certain safeguards, (6) could it be safely entrusted; (7) if Prebendary Scrivener were "guiding" the research; (8) and only when these men were unanimous on a point; (9) *"materially erred"* indicates that there might be a slight, unimportant error possible, but not gross error; (10) previous implies prior study of these matters; (11) *"life-long familiarity"* with textual criticism is needed; (12) or at least leisure for studying these matters ten or twenty years; (13) and this 10-20 year study must be *"with undivided attention"*; and (14) these safeguards were only to be desiderated (or "desired" or "wished for") rather than really looked for and found among all of the English divines in Dean Burgon's day.

The question that faces us in our day is this: if Dean Burgon couldn't find men in England in his own day, when Greek and Hebrew study was at its very pinnacle, how could we find such today, when the entire level and quality of education and training in these fields (or any others, for that matter) are at such a low ebb? Where could we find those who had an *"undivided attention"*? Consider television which makes "undivided attention" difficult. The members of our family could do the same things. Dean Burgon himself was not married and so did not have this kind of distraction. Where are the *"eight"* today with a *"life-long familiarity with the science of textual criticism"*? Where are the men who have *"ten or twenty years with absolutely undivided attention"* to undertake such a thorough-going study? The answer is, in my opinion, if such men who meet each and every one of these previous **14 prerequisites** are alive today, I would like to meet them. And yet, I do not believe that we can afford to cut a single one of these **14 prerequisites** down from Dean Burgon's high standard. Produce your men and produce the *"guidance"* from a current variety of Prebendary Scrivener's standing and scholarly ability (**if** one can be found), and then and only then, will I agree that we are ready for revision of the Textus Receptus of the Greek New Testament.

11. Dean Burgon Boldly Stated That Any "Authoritative Revision of the Greek Text" Must Precede Any "Future Revision of the English" Text of the New Testament, and "For Such an Undertaking" the "Time Has Not Yet Come." Dean Burgon wrote:

> Enough has been offered by this time to prove that an authoritative revision of the Greek text will have to precede any future revision of the English of the New Testament. Equally certain is it that for such an undertaking the time has not yet come. "It is my honest conviction," (remarks Bp. Ellicott, the Chairman of the revisionists,)--"that for any authoritative revision, we are not yet mature: either in Biblical learning or Hellenistic scholarship." [Dean Burgon, *Revision Revised,* p. 124.]

Even the Chairman of the English Revised Version (E.R.V.) Committee of 1881, Bishop Ellicott, agreed that they weren't ready for an *"authoritative revision"* because of a lack of *"Biblical learning"* and *"Hellenistic scholarship."*

12. Dean Burgon Laid Down Even More Specific Things That Had to Precede the Major Revision of the "Textus Receptus" and Prepare the Revisers for This Tedious Task. Since there are so very many details under this caption, we will break it down by separate headings.

a.   Dean Burgon Said That Although There Are "More Manuscripts" Then Available For Study, "Who Knows How to Use Them?" Dean Burgon wrote:

> True, that we enjoy access to--suppose from 1000 to 2000-- more manuscripts than were available when the Textus Receptus was formed. But nineteen-twentieths of these documents for any use which has been made of them, might just as well be still lying in the monastic libraries from which they were obtained.--true, that four out of our five oldest uncials have

come to light since the year1628, but who knows how to use them? [Dean Burgon, *Revision Revised, op. cit.* , p. 124.]

Dean Burgon pointed out what is perfectly clear to all thinking people, that is, even though there are thousands of manuscripts now available (as there were then available in Dean Burgon's day) what value are there if few (if any) either know how to use them or else refuse to use them, (like the Westcott and Hort devotees refuse to use the thousands of Textus Receptus manuscripts)?

b. Dean Burgon Pointed Out That the "Ancient Versions"Are of No Use Unless Men Come Forward To "Tell Us What They All Contain." Dean Burgon wrote:

> True, that we have made acquaintance with certain ancient versions about which little or nothing was known 200 years ago: but,--(with the solitary exception of the Rev. Solomon Caesar Malan, the learned Vicar of Broadwindsor,--who, by the way is always ready to lend a torch to his benighted brethren,)--what living Englishman is able to tell us what they all contain? A smattering acquaintance with the languages of ancient Egypt--the Gothic, Aethiopic, Armenian, Georgian and Slavonian versions,-- is of no manner of avail. In no department, probably, is "a little learning" more sure to prove "a dangerous thing." [Dean Burgon, *Revision Revised,* pp. 124-25.]

Again, what value are the discovery of many "ancient versions" of the New Testament into other languages unless there are people who are thoroughly trained and skilled in those languages who are able to *"tell us what they all contain."*

c. Dean Burgon Lamented the Fact That, Though "The Fathers" Have Been "Better Edited" Yet They Have Not Been Satisfactorily "Indexed." Dean Burgon wrote:

> True, lastly, that the Fathers have been better edited within the last 250 years: during which period some fresh Patristic writings have also come to light. But, with the exception of Theodoret among the Greeks and Tertullian among the Latins, which of the Fathers has been satisfactorily indexed? [Dean Burgon, *Revision Revised,* p. 125]

Here, Dean Burgon was calling for a "satisfactory index" of all the Fathers with Scriptural quotations all organized so that the textual critic might use it for research on exactly which text these Fathers had before them as they quoted, referred to, or used from memory. Dean Burgon's own index to the

Scriptural quotations of the Church Fathers in various colors is an excellent step toward the fulfillment of this requirement.

Perhaps it should be published and made available for scholars of the text of Scripture. Presently it is in the British Museum, unused, for the most part, and unavailable to the many who should have immediate and convenient access to it for work on various verses of the Bible. Dr. Jack Moorman, a Baptist missionary in England, as well as a member of our Dean Burgon Society Executive Committee, visited the British Museum and told me that because of the color-coding used by Dean Burgon, the indexes could not satisfactorily be published unless they were photographed in full color which would be very expensive. In addition to this, permission might not be granted by the British Museum for the project. It would also be difficult if not impossible to come up with the exact editions of the Church Fathers to which Dean Burgon was referring.

> **d.   Dean Burgon Decried the Fact That the "Fundamental Principles of the Science of Textual Criticism" Were "Not Yet Comprehended" and Called For a "Generation of Students" Who Would Give Themselves Up to This Neglected Branch of Sacred Science**. He wrote:

> The fundamental principles of the science of textual criticism are not yet apprehended. . . . let a generation of students give themselves entirely up to this neglected branch of Sacred science. [Dean Burgon, *Revision Revised,* p. 125.]

Dean Burgon here showed the need for students of these *"fundamental principles"* of *"the science of textual criticism"* such as Dean Burgon himself held to. Where are these students today? Where is one generation of them? Where are those men who have *"given themselves entirely up to this neglected branch of Sacred science"*?

> **e.   Dean Burgon's Other Prerequisites for Sound Textual Criticism:**

> **(1) We Need at Least "500 More Copies" of the New Testament "Diligently Collated."** Dean Burgon wrote:

> Let 500 more copies of the Gospels, Acts, and Epistles be diligently collated. [Dean Burgon, *Revision Revised,* p. 125.]

Has this yet been done? No, it has not.

> **(2) We Need At Least "100" "Ancient Lectionaries" "Very Exactly Collated."** Dean Burgon wrote:

> Let at least 100 of the ancient Lectionaries be very exactly

collated also. [Dean Burgon, *Revision Revised,* p. 125.]
Has this yet been done? No, it has not.

(3) We Need the "Most Important Ancient Versions" To Be "Edited Afresh"and Let Their "Languages" Be "Really Mastered by Englishmen." Dean Burgon wrote:

> Let the most important of the ancient versions be edited afresh and let the languages in which these are written be for the first time really mastered by Englishmen. [Dean Burgon, *Revision Revised,* p. 125.]

Has this yet been done? No, it has not.

(4) We Need, "Above All," the Church "Fathers" to Yield "Their Precious Secrets" by "Ransacking" Them, "Indexing" Them, And "Diligently Inspecting" Them. Dean Burgon wrote:

> Above all let the Fathers be called upon to give up their precious secrets. Let their writings be ransacked and indexed, and (where needful) let the MSS. of their works be diligently inspected in order that we may know what actually is the evidence which they afford. [Dean Burgon, *Revision Revised,* p. 125.]

Has this yet been done? No, it has not.

f.   Dean Burgon's Conclusion As to the Importance of These Four Preceding Suggestions. Dean Burgon wrote:

> Only so will it ever be possible to obtain a Greek text on which absolute reliance may be placed and which may serve as the basis for a satisfactory revision of our Authorized Version. [Dean Burgon, *Revision Revised, op., cit.*, p. 125.]

Dean Burgon, by this quotation, stressed the importance he placed on (1) copies; (2) Lectionaries; (3) versions; and (4) Fathers in his valid principles of textual criticism that would yield beyond all question what actually were the precise and exact Words of Scripture in the originals. You will also note that he opposed any *"revision"* in any manner of the King James Bible until all of his prerequisites for the Greek New Testament were fulfilled.

g.   Dean Burgon Also Suggested That "Unpublished Works of the Ancient Greek Fathers" Should Be "Printed." Dean Burgon wrote:

> Nay, let whatever unpublished works of the ancient Greek Fathers are anywhere known to exist,--(and not a few precious

remains of theirs are lying hid in great national libraries, both at
home and abroad,)--let these be printed. The men could easily
be found: the money, far more easily. . . . [Dean Burgon,
Revision Revised, pp. 125-26.]

Has this yet been done? No, it has not.

**13. Dean Burgon Maintained That "For the First
Time," "the Science of Textual Criticism" Must Be
Prosecuted "in a Scholarlike Manner."** Dean Burgon wrote:

Yes, and in the meantime--(Let it in all faithfulness be added)--
the science of textual criticism will have to be prosecuted, for
the first time, in a scholarlike manner. Fundamental principles--
sufficiently axiomatic to ensure general acceptance,--will have to
be laid down for man's guidance. The time has quite gone by
for vaunting "the now established principles of textual criticism,"--as if they had an actual existence. Let us be shown,
instead, which those principles be. As for the weak superstition
of these last days, which--without proof of any kind--would
erect two IVth-century copies of the New Testament (dem-
onstrably derived from one and the same utterly depraved
archetype,) into an authority from which there shalt be no
appeal,--it cannot be too soon or too unconditionally abandoned. [Dean Burgon, *Revision Revised,* pp. 227-28]

Dean Burgon therefore wished to *"abandon"* once and for all the shallow,
unscholarlike presuppositions--wholly without proof of any kind--foisted
upon the Christian world by those religious apostates and heretics, Westcott
and Hort. Dean Burgon considered these *"two IVth-century copies"* ("B"
and "Aleph") to be like Israel's two "golden calves."

**14. Dean Burgon Wished to See God's "Highly
Complex Provision" For the "Effectual Conservation" of
His "Crowning Master-Piece"--the Written Word--"Duly
Considered."** Dean Burgon wrote:

For, let the ample and highly complex provision which Divine
wisdom hath made for the effectual conservation of that
crowning master-piece of his own creative skill,--the written
Word,--be duly considered. [Dean Burgon, *Revision Revised,*
p. 338.]

What Dean Burgon was saying in this quotation, was that we should not
neglect any facet whatsoever of God's *"ample and highly complex
provision"* for the *"conservation"* of his *"written Word,"* but should study
all the evidence, including: (1) copies; (2) versions; (3) Lectionaries; and
(4) Church Fathers in an effort to arrive at exactly what word was in the

autographs of the New Testament.

15. Dean Burgon Laid Down the Only "Trust- worthy Method" in "Ascertaining the Truth of Scripture." Dean Burgon wrote:

> A safer, the only trustworthy method, in fact, of ascertaining the truth of Scripture, we hold to be the method which, without prejudice or partiality, simply ascertains which form of the text enjoys the earliest, the fullest, the widest, the most respectable, and--above all things--the most varied attestation, that a reading should be freely recognized alike by the earliest and by the latest available evidence,--we hold to be a prime circumstance in its favour. That copies, versions, and Fathers, should all three concur in sanctioning it,--we hold to be even more conclusive. If several fathers, living in different parts of ancient Christen- dom, are all observed to recognize the words, or to quote them in the same way,--we have met with all the additional confirm- ation we ordinarily require. [Dean Burgon, *Revision Revised,* pp. 339-40.]

This method of Dean Burgon is a far cry from the unsatisfactory, slip-shod, "guess-work" methodology of Westcott and Hort and their present progeny of textual critics.

16. Dean Burgon Affirmed That a Trustworthy "Textual Critic" Must Have a "Clear Head" and a "Calm, Dispassionate Judgment." In speaking against the wrong charac- teristics of a Textual Critic, Dean Burgon touched on the real requirements:

> The spectacle of an able and estimable man exhibiting such singular inaptitude for a province of study which, beyond all others, demands a clear head and a calm, dispassionate judg- ment--creates distress. (Dean Burgon, *Revision Revised,* p. 394.]

These are important qualifications of the would-be "textual critic."

17. Dean Burgon Stated Clearly That There Could Be "No Compromise" Between the "New German System" Used by Westcott and Hort and the "Old Eng- lish School of Textual Criticism" Adopted by Dean Bur- gon and Others Because They Are "Antagonistic Throughout." Dean Burgon wrote:

> . . . it cannot be too plainly stated that no compromise is possible between our respective methods.,--yours and mine: [that is, Bishop Ellicott, Chairman of the E.R.V. committee, who used the same methods as Westcott and Hort who were also on

that committee] between the new German system in its most aggravated and in fact intolerable form to which you have incautiously and unconditionally given in your adhesion; and the old English school of textual criticism of which I humbly avow myself a disciple. Between the theory of Drs. Westcott and Hort (which you have made your own) and the method of your present respondent, there can be no compromise, because the two are antagonistic throughout. We have, in fact, nothing in common,,--except certain documents; which I insist on interpreting by the humble inductive process: while you and your friends insist on your right of deducing your estimate of them from certain antecedent imaginations of your own,--every one of which I disallow, and some of which I am able to disprove.
[Dean Burgon, *Revision Revised, op. cit.*, p. 517.]

Dean Burgon saw no truce in this battle of methods in textual criticism-- between the *"new German system"* and the *"old English school."*

18. Dean Burgon Laid Down His Method As One of "Humility" and "Self-Renouncing Labour" While Inspecting "the Best Copies, Fathers, Versions."

Dean Burgon wrote to Ellicott, as a representative of the Westcott and Hort school of methodology:

You assume that you possess a power of divination which enables you to dispense with laborious processes of induction while I, on the contrary, insist that the truth of the text of Scripture is to be elicited exclusively from the consentient testimony of the largest number of the best copies, Fathers, versions. There is, I am persuaded, no royal road to the attainment of truth in this department of knowledge. Only through the lowly portal of humility--only by self-renouncing labour--may we ever hope to reach the innermost shrine.
[Dean Burgon, *Revision Revised,* p. 518.]

This sounds like work, work, and more work. And it is. Perhaps this is why it has not been undertaken in the manner in which Dean Burgon specified.

19. Dean Burgon Set Forth Three "Test Places" to Test Out His Sound Methods Versus Westcott and Hort's Fallacious and Unsound Methods: (1) "the Last Twelve Verses of Mark" (2) "the Angelic Hymn" of Luke 2:14; and (3) 1 Timothy 3:16.

Dean Burgon wrote:

Let me be allowed, in conclusion, to recommend to your attention and that of your friends:--(i.) "The Last Twelve Verses of S. Mark's gospel:--(ii.) the angelic hymn on the night of the Nativity:--(iii.) the text of I Timothy iii.16--these three--(in respect of which up to this hour, you and I find ourselves to be hopelessly divided,)--as convenient test places. When you are prepared frankly to admit:--(I.) that there is no reason whatever for doubting the genuineness of S. Mark xvi. 9-20:--(ii.) that εν ανθρωποις ευδοκια is unquestionably the Evangelical text of S. Luke ii.14:--and (iii.) that θεος εφανερωθη εν σαρκι is what the great Apostle must be held to have written in I Timothy iii.16--we shall be in good time to proceed to something else. Until this happy result has been attained, it is a mere waste of time to break up fresh ground, and to extend the area of our differences. [Dean Burgon, *Revision Revised,* p. 519.]

This is a very important statement to understand from Dean Burgon. These three passages are of crucial importance in understanding the different methods espoused by Dean John William Burgon, and those of Westcott and Hort and company. Dean Burgon has splendidly exhonorated the Traditional Text in all three of these places in *Revision Revised* for all to see [Cf. pp. 36-40; 41-47; 47-49; 98-106; and 420-501].

III.
DEAN JOHN BURGON'S WARN-
INGS CONCERNING REVISION OF
THE ENGLISH KING JAMES
(AUTHORIZED) BIBLE

Having discussed Dean Burgon's prerequisites and **WARNINGS** regarding the major revision of the Greek Text of the New Testament, we now come to the second major portion of this study, that is, under what conditions would Dean Burgon suggest that a major relision be undertaken (if any) of the English in the King James (Authorized) Bible. With a rash of "new versions" and perversions continuing to pour out of the publishing houses during the 20th century and no doubt into the 21st century, and with Dean Burgon being misquoted by those who differ from him on this matter, it is of the utmost importance to see what this man thought about English translations in general, as well as the King James (Authorized) Bible. We will examine three major areas in this section: (1) Dean Burgon's assessment of the faults of the English Revised Version (E.R.V.); (2) Dean Burgon's assessment of the excellency of the King James (Authorized) Bible (KJB/AV); and (3) Dean Burgon's suggestions concerning the time and conditions for any revision of the King James (Authorized) Bible in English, it at all.

A. Dean Burgon's Assessment of the Faults of the English Revised Version (E.R.V.) Though in this section Dean Burgon takes up the faults of the English Revised Version (E.R.V.) of 1881 which was based on the Westcott and Hort Greek text, the same things could be said of many other English Translations based on that same text which have been produced since that time.

1. Dean Burgon Felt That the "English"of the "Newly Revised Version" (E.R.V. of 1881) Was "Hopelessly at Fault." Dean Burgon wrote:

> The English, (as well as the Greek) of the newly "Revised Version" is hopelessly at fault. It is to me simply unintelligible

how a company of scholars can have spent ten years in
elaborating such a very unsatisfactory product. Their uncouth
phraseology and their jerky sentences, their pedantic obscurity
and their unidiomatic English, contrast painfully with "the happy
turns of expression, the music of the cadences, the felicities of
the rhythm" of our Authorized Version. The transition from
one to the other, as the Bishop of Lincoln remarks, is like
exchanging a well-built carriage for a vehicle without springs, in
which you get jolted to death on a newly-mended and rarely-
traversed road. But the "Revised Version" is inaccurate as well;
exhibits defective scholarship, I mean, in countless places. [Dean
Burgon, *Revision Revised,* p. vi.]

Dean Burgon has certainly zeroed in specifically on just exactly why he felt
the E.R.V. English was *"hopelessly at fault."* I wonder what he would have
thought of the much less well done "modern translations" such as the Living
Version, the New International Version, the New American Standard
Version, the New English Version, the Good News For Modern Man, and
similar editions? I feel strongly that he would have had as many harsh
words (and probably a great deal more) for these, as he found for the E.R.V.
of 1881.

**2.   Dean Burgon Branded the E.R.V. "Revised
Version" as Making the "Authorized English Bible" "Silently Revised."** Dean Burgon wrote:

. . . with some slight modifications, our Authorised English
Version has been silently revised: silently, I say, for in the margin
of the English no record is preserved of the underlying textual
changes which have been introduced by the revisionists. On the
contrary. Use has been made of that margin to insinuate suspicion and distrust in countless particulars as to the authenticity
of the text which has been suffered to remain unaltered. [Dean
Burgon, *Revision Revised, op. cit,* p. xxx.]

I am certain that Dean Burgon would have said the same thing about our
modern "English versions" as well.

**3.   Dean Burgon Pointed Out That the "English
Revised Version" of 1881 Was "Destined to Supersede
the "Authorized Bible of 1611."** Dean Burgon wrote:

Not unreasonable therefore is the expectation entertained by
its Authors that the "New English Version" founded on this
"new Greek text" is destined to supersede the "Authorized
Version" of 1611. [Dean Burgon, *Revision Revised, op. cit.,*
p.2.]

This same claim has been made by our modern English versions as well. As of now, the English Revised Version (E.R.V.) of 1881 has been dead and buried for decades, while the King James Bible lives on.

4.   Dean Burgon Charged the E.R.V. With "Blotting out" of the Bible "Many Precious Words" Which the Mere English Reader Could Not Know Of Their "Existence." Dean Burgon wrote:

> We shall therefore pass on, when we have asked the revisionists in turn--how they have dared so effectually to blot out these many precious words from the Book of Life, that no mere English reader, depending on the Revised Version for his know-ledge of the Gospels, can by possibility suspect their existence? [Dean Burgon, *Revision Revised,* p. 118.]

This is the case with many modern versions as well. Check Mark 16:9-20 for example, 1 Timothy 3:16, and John 7:53--8:11, and you will see, in just about all of the so-called "modern versions" of the New Testament, there is a questioning of these verses in some or many respects. Dr. Jack Moorman has come up with a total of 356 doctrinal passages where the Westcott and Hort text departs from the Textus Receptus underlying the King James Bible. Some of these important doctrines are missing without a trace in the English. [See **B.F.T. #1825 @ $15+S&H,** *Early Manuscripts and The Authorized Version--A Closer Look*.] He also found that the Westcott and Hort text was 2,886 words **shorter** than the Textus Receptus. When these words are dropped out, in many instances, there is no trace of their being missing. [See **B.F.T. #1726 @ $8+S&H,** *Missing in Modern Versions--Is the Full Story Being Told?*] This is the kind of thing Dean Burgon was alluding to above.

5.   Dean Burgon Compared the KJB With the New E.R.V. and Agreed That "the Old Is Better." Dean Burgon wrote:

> Thus it happens that we never spend half-an-hour over the un-fortunate production before us [i.e. the E.R.V. of 1881] without exclaiming (with one in the Gospel),"the old is better." Changes of any sort are unwelcome in such a book as the Bible; but the discovery that changes have been made for the worse offends greatly. [Dean Burgon, *Revision Revised,* p. 144.]

Again, the same can be said of modern "versions" and "perversions" of the Bible.

6.   Dean Burgon Charged the E.R.V. Translators With "an Imperfect Acquaintance with the Genius of the Greek Language" and Only a "Moderate" Appreciation

for English. Dean Burgon wrote:

> We regret to discover that, in both respects [i.e. rendering of Greek tenses and of the definite article], their work is disfigured throughout by changes which convict a majority of their body alike of an imperfect acquaintance with the genius of the Greek language, and of scarcely a moderate appreciation of the idiomatic proprieties of their own. [Dean Burgon, *Revision Revised,* p. 154.]

Compare our modern versions with this comment, and you will find much that is similar.

7.   Dean Burgon Castigated the E.R.V. Revisionists as Using "Schoolboy Methods," of Not Being "Masters of Their Own Language," and of Parting Company With "William Tyndale" and the "Giants"Who Gave Us Our Authorized Version." Dean Burgon wrote:

> But what supremely annoys us in the work just now under review is, that the schoolboy method of translation already noticed is therein exhibited in constant operation throughout. It becomes oppressive. We are never permitted to believe that we are in the company of scholars who are altogether masters of their own language.   Their solicitude ever seems to be twofold:--(1) to exhibit a singular indifference to the proprieties of English speech, while they maintain a servile adherence (etymological or idiomatic, as the case may be) to the Greek:-- (2) right or wrong, to part company from William Tyndale and the giants who gave us our "Authorized Version." [Dean Burgon, *Revision Revised,* p. 155.]

A mastery of English is the very first qualification for any English translator.

8.   Dean Burgon Had High Praise For the "Real Genius" of "William Tyndale" in Opposition to "Men of 1881." Dean Burgon wrote:

> . . . the plain fact being that the men of 1611--above all, that William Tyndale 77 years before them--produced a work of real genius; seizing with generous warmth the meaning and intention of the sacred writers, and perpetually varying the phrase, as they felt or fancied that Evangelists and Apostles would have varied it, had they had to express themselves in English: whereas the men of 1881 have fulfilled their task in what can only be described as a spirit of servile pedantry. The grammarian (pure and simple) crops up everywhere. We seem never to rise

above the atmosphere of the lecture-room. [Dean Burgon, *Revision Revised,* p. 167.]

The King James Bible truly is a *"work of real genius."*

9. Dean Burgon Chided the E.R.V. Revisionists for the "Mistaken Principle" of Trying to Translate the "Same Greek Word by the Same English Word." Dean Burgon wrote:

> We must needs advert again to the ominous admission made in the Revisionists' Preface (iii.2 init.) that to some extent they recognized the duty of a "rigid adherence to the rule of translating, as far as possible, the same Greek word by the same English word." This mistaken principle of theirs lies at the root of so much of the mischief which has befallen the Authorized Version. . . . the"translators" of 1611, towards the close of their long and quaint address "to the reader," offer the following statement concerning what had been their ownpractice:--"we have not tied ourselves" (say they) "to an uniformity of phrasing, or to an identity of words, as some peradventure would wish that we had done." On this, they presently enlarge. We have been "especially careful," have even "made a conscience," "not to vary from the sense of that which we had translated before, if the word signified the same thing in both places." But then, (as they shrewdly point out in passing,) "there be some words that be not of the same sense everywhere. . . ."if" (say they,) "we translate the Hebrew or Greek word once purpose never to call it intent; if one were journeying, never travelling if one were think, never suppose; if one were pain, never ache, if one were joy, never gladness;--thus to mince the matter, we thought to savour more of curiosity than of wisdom." [Dean Burgon, *Revision Revised,* p. 187-88.]

This is an important principle to note. Where Hebrew or Greek words have various senses, then certainly the context must determine. There must not be a slavish adherence to sameness or identical wording unless clearly indicated by the context. To do this would be to abolish the fineness of distinctness and taste of the English idiom.

10. Dean Burgon Gave a Devastating "Put-Down" of the E.R.V. Revisionists' Work as "Singularly Deficient" in Every Way Imaginable. Dean Burgon wrote:

> Even this, however, is not nearly all. As Translators. full two-thirds of the revisionists have shown themselves singularly de-ficient,--alike in their critical acquaintance with the language out

of which they had to translate, and in their familiarity with the
idiomatic requirements of their own tongue. They had a noble
version before them, which they have contrived to spoil in
every part. Its dignified simplicity and essential faithfulness, its
manly grace and its delightful rythm, they have shown themselves alike unable to imitate and unwilling to retain. Their
queer uncouth phraseology and their jerky sentences:--their
pedantic obscurity and their stiff, constrained manner:--their
fidgetty affectation of accuracy;--and their habitual achievement
of English which fails to exhibit the spirit of the original Greek;--
are sorry substitutes for the living freshness, and elastic freedom, and habitual fidelity of the Grand Old Version which we
inherited from our fathers, and which has sustained the spiritual
life of the church of England, and of all English-speaking Christians. for 350 years. . . .--the Authorized Version, wherever it
was possible, should have been jealously retained. But on the
contrary. Every familiar cadence has been dislocated: the con-
genial flow of almost every verse of Scripture has been hopelessly marred: so many of those little connecting words, which
give life and continuity to a narrative, have been vexatiously
displaced, that a perpetual sense of annoyance is created. The
countless minute alterations which have been needlessly introduced into every familiar page prove at last as tormenting as a
swarm of flies to the weary traveller on a summer's day. To
speak plainly, the book has been made unreadable. . . . we lay
the revisers' volume down convinced that the case of the work
is simply hopeless. [Dean Burgon, *Revision Revised,* pp. 225-
26]

These are very descriptive phrases which Dean Burgon has woven into his
critique of the E.R.V. He has illustrated them throughout his volume.

   **11. Dean Burgon Advised That the Entire E.R.V.
Be "Ploughed Up" and let the "Ground" Alone For a "Decent Space of Time Without Cultivation."** Dean Burgon
wrote:

Had the blemishes been capable of being reckoned up, it might
have been worthwhile to try to remedy some of them. But
when instead of being disfigured by a few weeds scattered here
and there, the whole field proves to be sown over in every
direction with thorns and briars; above all when, deep beneath
the surface, roots of bitterness to be counted by thousands, are
found to have been silently planted in, which are sure to

produce poisonous fruit after many days:--under such circumstances only one course can be prescribed. Let the entire area
be ploughed up;--ploughed deep; and let the ground be left for
a decent space of time without cultivation. It is idle--worse than
idle--to dream of revising, with a view to retaining, this Revision.
[Dean Burgon, *Revision Revised,* p. 227.]

Dean Burgon held out no hope whatsoever for salvaging the English
Revised Version (E..R.V.),so vile was it in its renderings, style, and in every
other way.

**12. Dean Burgon Looked at the E.R.V. as a "Text
Book" for Teachers to Instruct Their Pupils "to Beware
of the Textual Errors of the Revisionists of 1881."** Dean
Burgon wrote:

Their well-meant endeavours have provided an admirable text-
book for teachers of divinity,--who will henceforth instruct their
pupils to **beware** of the textual errors of the Revisionists of
1881, as well as their tasteless, injudicious, and unsatisfactory
essays in translation. This work of theirs will discharge the office of a **WARNING** beacon to as many as shall hereafter
embark on the same perlious enterprise with themselves. It will
convince men of the danger of pursuing the same ill-omened
course: trusting to the same unskilful guidance, venturing too
near the same wreck-strewn shore. [Dean Burgon, *Revision
Revised,* pp. 231-32]

I wonder if the current lot of "translators" have profited as much as they
should have from the dangers of the E.R.V. work? I think not.

**13. Dean Burgon Branded the E.R.V. Work as
"Tasteless, Unlovely, Harsh, Unidiomatic:--Servile Without Being Really Faithful."** Dean Burgon wrote:

. . . how it happened that--, with so many splendid scholars sit-
ting round their table, that they should have produced a
translation which, for the most part, reads like a first-rate
school-boy's crib, unlovely, harsh, unidiomatic;--servile without
being really faithful,--pedantic without being really learned;--
unreadable translation, in short; the result of a vast amount of
labour indeed, but of wondrous little skill:--how all this has
come about, it were utterly useless at this time of day to en-
quire. [Dean Burgon, *Revision Revised,* p. 238]

This certainly sums up Dean Burgon's misgivings about the E.R.V.

**14. Dean Burgon Quoted With Approval Bishop
Wordsworth's Criticisms of the E.R.V.** Dean Burgon wrote,

quoting Wordsworth:

"I fear we must say in candour that in the Revised Version we meet in every page with small changes, which are vexations, teasing, and irritating, even the more so because they are small; which seem almost to be made for the sake of change." Bishop Wordsworth. [Dean Burgon, *Revision Revised,* p. 368.]

Dean Burgon was not the only one of his time to be disappointed in the work of the E.R.V.Translators.

B.   Dean Burgon's High Esteem for the Authorized (King James) Bible of 1611. Along with the above quotations giving Dean Burgon's disdain for the English Revised Version (E.R.V.) of 1881, we must realize that he held in very high esteem the marvelous work of the King James (Authorized) Bible translators of 1611. Some of the quotations will be given below in support of this.

1.   Dean Burgon Compared the K.J.B. & the E.R.V. to a Ride Down a "Newly-Mended" Road. Dean Burgon wrote:

. . . and their unidiomatic English, [of the E.R.V.] contrast painfully with"the happy turns of expression, the music of the cadences, the felicities of the rhythm" of our Authorized Version. The transition from one to the other, as the Bishop of Lincoln remarks, is like exchanging a well-built carriage for a vehicle without springs, in which you get jolted to death on a newly-mended and rarety-traversed road.   [Dean Burgon, *Revision Revised,* p. vi.]

Dean Burgon's admiration for the King James Bible's New Testament is clear from this quotation.

2.   Dean Burgon Highly Praised the Authorized Bible as the "Noblest Literary Work in the Anglo-Saxon Language" and that "No 'Revision'" Can Match Its Esteem. Dean Burgon wrote:

Whatever may be urged in favour of Biblical revision, it is at least undeniable that the undertaking involves a tremendous risk. Our Authorized Version is the one religious link which at present binds together ninety millions of English-speaking men scattered over the earth's surface. Is it reasonable that so un-utterably precious, so sacred a bond should be endangered, for the sake of representing certain words more accuratety,--here and there translating a tense with greater precision,--getting rid of a few archaisms? It may be confidently assumed that no 'revision' of our authorized version, however judiciously executed, will ever occupy the place in public esteem which is actually enjoyed by the work of the translators of 1611,--the noblest literary work in the Anglo-Saxon language. [Dean Burgon, *Revision Revised,* p. 113.]

Dean Burgon is sceptical that any *"revision"* can take the place *"in public esteem"* as the New Testament occupied. Is this also true in our own day? It certainly is!

3.   Dean Burgon Held the "Old" KJB to Be "Better" Than the New E.R.V. Dean Burgon wrote:

Thus it happens that we never spend half-an-hour over the unfortunate production before us [i.e., the E.R.V. of 1881] exclaiming (with one in the Gospel), "the old is better." [Dean Burgon, *Revision Revised,* p. 145]

Truly the "old" King James (Authorized) Bible is better than all of the versions and perversions that have been made before or since.

4.   Dean Burgon Held That the "Men of 1611" Produced "a Work of Real Genius." Dean Burgon wrote:

. . . the plain fact being that the men of 1611--above all that William Tyndale 77 years before them---produced a work of real genius; seizing with generous warmth the meaning and intention of the Sacred writers, and perpetually varying the phrase, as they felt or fancied that Evangelists and Apostles would have varied it, had they had to express themselves in English: . . . [Dean Burgon, *Revision Revised,* p. 167.]

How much Dean Burgon appreciated the Authorized Bible of 1611!

5.   Dean Burgon Mentioned the "Great Scholars of 1611" and Their "Profound Consciousness of the Use of the Greek Word, "*Aitein.*" Dean Burgon wrote:

The verb **aitein** confessedly means "to ask." And perhaps no better general English equivalent could be suggested for it. But then, In a certain context, "ask" would be an inadequate rendering: in another, it would be improper; in a third, it would be simply intolerable. Of all this, the great scholars of 1611 showed themselves profoundly conscious. . . . [Dean Burgon, *Revision Revised,* p. 190.]

Dean Burgon then illustrated this point in the context of this chapter.

6.   Dean Burgon Stated That the KJB Translators "Understood Their Craft" Because "the Spirit of Their God Was Mightily Upon Them." Dean Burgon wrote:

. . . who does not respond gratefully to the exquisite taste and tact with which "bondmaid" itself has been exchanged for

"bondwoman" by our translators of 1611, in verses 23, 30 and
31 . . . verily, those men understood their craft! "There were
giants in those days." As little would they submit to be bound
by the new cords of the Philistines as by their green withes.
Upon occasion, they could shake themselves free from either.
And why? For the selfsame reason: viz. Because the Spirit of
their God was mightily upon them. [Dean Burgon, *Revision
Revised,* p. 196.]

    **7.   Dean Burgon Praised the KJB Greatly Over
the E.R.V. as Being "a Noble Version" With "Dignified
Simplicity," "Essential Faithfulness," "Manly Grace,"
and "Delightful Rhythm."** Dean Burgon wrote:

They held a noble version before them, [the King James Bible]
which they contrived to spoil in every part. Its dignified
simplicity and essential faithfulness, its manly grace and its
delightful rhythym, they have shown themselves alike unable to
imitate and unwilling to retain. . . . are sorry substitutes for the
living freshness, and elastic freedom, and habitual fidelity of the
grand old version which we inherited from our fathers, and
which has sustained the spiritual life of the church of England,
and of all English-speaking Christians, for 350 years. . . . the
Authorized Version, wherever it was possible, should have been
jealously retained, . . . (Dean Burgon, *Revision Revised,* pp. 225-
26.]

    **8.   Dean Burgon Called The KJB a "Priceless
Treasure" Which Is "Faithful and Trustworthy."** Dean
Burgon wrote:

. . . It will teach faithful hearts to cling the closer to the priceless
treasure which was bequeathed to them by the piety and wisdom
of their fathers. It will dispel for ever the dream of those who
have secretly imagined that a more exact version, undertaken
with the boasted helps of this nineteenth century of ours would
bring to light something which has been hitherto unfairly kept
concealed or else misrepresented. Not the least service which
the revisionists have rendered has been the proof their work
affords, how very seldom our Authorized Version is materially
wrong; how faithful and trustworthy, on the contrary, it is
throughout. [Dean Burgon, *Revision Revised,* p. 232.]

From the above quotations, there can be no doubt whatsoever about Dean
John William Burgon's high praise for and confidence in the King James
(Authorized) Bible of 1611. This confidence and praise, on Dean Burgon's

part, was not born of ignorance, but of vast knowledge about the subject under consideration, together with the many long hours of research and study of the Bible

C.   Dean Burgon's Suggestions as to When a Major Revision of the KJB Should Begin and What Things Must Needs Precede Such Revision. Dean Burgon was not a man who would cascade out of control into something that he felt must eventually be undertaken. On the contrary, he reasoned out thoroughly the timing of such a move, as well as the details of how best to carry it out.

1.   Dean Burgon Was Unshakable in His Belief That "an Authoritative Revision of the Greek Text Must "Precede Any Future Revision of the English of the New Testament." Dean Burgon wrote:

> Enough has been offered by this time to prove that an authoritative revision of the Greek text will have to precede any future revision of the English of the New Testament. [Dean Burgon, *Revision Revised,* p. 124]

In other words, until an *"authoritative revision"* of the Greek text is made to conform it with **all** of his prerequisites, Dean Burgon was dead set against any *"future revision of the English of the New Testament."*   To this day, **this has not been done.**

2.   Dean Burgon Was Also Firm in His Belief That Even in His Own Times "the Time Has Not Yet Come," Because of an Immaturity in "Biblical Learning" or "Hellenistic Scholarship." Burgon wrote:

> Equally certain is it that for such an undertaktng [i.e. a "future revision" of the English New Testament], the time has not yet come. "It is my honest conviction,"--(remarks Bp. Ellicott, the Chairman of the Revisionists,)--"that for any authoritative revision, we are not yet mature; either in Biblical learning or Hellenistic scholarship." [Dean Burgon, *Revision Revised,* p. 124.]

Dean Burgon outlined (cf. pp. 124-126) in the most minute detail the various requirements necessary for a proper revision of the Greek text which would then form the basis for a satisfactory revision of our "Authorized Bible." He wrote:

> Only so will it ever be possible to obtain a Greek text on which absolute reliance may be placed, and which may serve as the basis for a satisfactory revision of our Authorized Version. . . . when all this has been done,--not before--then in God's Name, let the church address herself to the great undertaking.

[Dean Burgon, *Revision Revised,* p. 126.]

3.   Dean Burgon Plead For "Time" to Be Given After the E.R.V. "Revision" and"Textual Criticism" Must Have Been Pursued in a "Scholarlike Manner." Burgon wrote:

> Let the entire area be ploughed up,--ploughed deep; and let the ground be left for a decent space of time without cultivation. It is idle---worse than idle--to dream of revising, with a view to retaining, this revision. Another generation of students must be suffered to arise. Time must be given for passion and prejudice to cool effectually down. Partizanship, (which at present prevails to an extraordinary extent, but which is wondrously out of place in this department of sacred learning,)--partizanship must be completely outlived,--before the church can venture, with the remotest prospect of a successful issue, to organize another attempt at revising the Authorized Version of the New Testament Scriptures. Yes, and in the meantime-(let it in all faithfulness be added)--the science of textual criticism will have to be prosecuted, for the first time, in a scholarlike manner. [Dean Burgon, *Revision Revised,* p. 227.]

The *"scholarlike manner"* of which Dean Burgon wrote, would be that manner which followed Dean Burgon's suggestions and **WARNINGS** concerning Textual Criticism. Such has not been the case, however. Publishers and writers have failed to heed Dean Burgon's clear **WARNINGS** on revision.

D.   Dean Burgon's Suggestions as to Principles of Translation Which Should Prevail for Any "Revision" of the King James (Authorized) Bible. Should the other provisions of Dean Burgon be fulfilled such as are listed above, he then laid down certain suggestions and **WARNINGS** for any *"revision"* of the King James (Authorized) Version of the Bible which he felt must be followed if it were to be successful.

1.   Dean Burgon Felt Any "Revised Edition of the Authorized Version" Should Be Only as a "Companion in the Study" and for "Private Edification" as a "Reference for Critical Purposes" Regarding "Difficult" or "Controverted Passages." Dean Burgon wrote:

> To be brief,--As a companion in the study and for private edification: as a book of reference for critical purposes, especially in respect of difficult and controverped passages:--we hold that a revised edition of the Authorized Version of our English

Bible, . . [Dean Burgon, *Revision Revised,* pp. 113-14.]
Note that this is not for *"public"* use instead of the New Testament, *but "in the study"* and for *"private"* edification as a *"reference."*

2.   Dean Burgon Stated That Any Such Revised Edition" of the A.V. Would Have To Be "Executed with Consummate Ability and Learning." Dean Burgon wrote:

> . . . we hold that a Revised edition of the Authorized Version of our English Bible (if executed with consummate ability and learning,) would at any time be a work of inestimable value. [Dean Burgon, *Revision Revised, op. cit.,* p. 114.]

The *"consummate ability and learning"* is a key factor to any proposed *"revised edition."*

3.   Dean Burgon Hesitated To Comment on the "Method" of Such "Revised Edition," Whether by "Marginal Notes" or in Some Other Way. Dean Burgon wrote:

> The method of such a performance, whether by marginal notes or in some other way, we forbear to determine. [Dean Burgon, *Revision Revised,* p. 114]

The use of *"marginal notes"* was suggested as one possible method, though not the only one.

4.   Dean Burgon Considered Such "Revised Edition" as Only a "Handmaid" of the A.V. But Not Something to "Supersede" It as a "Rival Translation" Which Was "Not to be Entertained for a Moment" But Was "Deprecated Entirely." Dean Burgon wrote:

> But certainly only as a handmaid is it to be desired. As something intended to supersede our present English Bible, we are thoroughly convinced that the project of a rival translation is not to be entertained for a moment. For ourselves, we deprecate it entirely. [Dean Burgon, *Revision Revised,* p. 114.]

These provisions are as equally important as the preceding ones, and should not be overlooked.

5.   Dean Burgon Felt the Greek Grammar Should "Give Way" to "English Idiom in Any Successful Translation. Dean Burgon wrote:

> There are laws of English idiom as well as laws of Greek grammar: and when these clash in what is meant to be a translation into English out of Greek, the latter must perforce give way to the former,--or we make ourselves ridiculous, and misrepresent what we purpose to translate. [Dean Burgon, *Revision Revised,* p.159.]

The E.R.V. of 1881 failed miserably in many instances, as Dean Burgon has shown.

6. Dean Burgon Pointed Out The "Difficulty" of "Translation" as Being "Most Subtle," and "Delicate."

Dean Burgon wrote:

> The truth is,--as all who have given real thought to the subject must be aware,--the phenomena of language are among the most subtle and delicate imaginable: the problem of translation, one of the most many sided and difficult that can be named. And if this holds universally, in how much greater a degree when the book to be translated is the Bible. [Dean Burgon, *Revision Revised*, p. 197.]

From this quotation, it would seem that Dean Burgon would not have someone plunge into the *"language"* translation of the Bible hurriedly, or without solid preparation and skill for it.

7.   Dean Burgon Also Mentioned That "Time" Must Be Given After the E.R.V. Attempt of 1881 So "Passion and Prejudice" Might Cool Down.

As was mentioned earlier, Dean Burgon wrote:

> . . . Another generation of students must be suffered to arise. Time must be given for passion and prejudice to cool effectually down.   Partizanship, (which at present prevails to an extraordinary extent, but which is wondrously out of place in this department of Sacred learning,)--partizanship must be completely outlived--before the church can venture, with the remotest prospect of a successful issue. to organize another attempt at revising the Authorized Version of the New Testament Scriptures. [Dean Burgon, *Revision Revised*, p. 227.]

Prejudice, passion and partizanship have no part in any genuine "revised edition" of the A.V. when all other factors are fulfilled.

IV.
SUMMARY AND CONCLUSIONS

A. Summary. Before giving some conclusions found in this brief study about Dean John William Dean Burgon's views on major revision of the Greek and English Bibles, I will summarize what has transpired briefly to this point in the paper.

1. Section one suggested six reasons for this study; desctibed how the study would be made; and gave the organization of the remainder of the study (pp. 1-4).

2. Section two dealt with Dean Dean Burgon's prerequisites for major revision of the New Testament Greek TEXTUS RECEPTUS. This was developed under four major headings: (1) Dean Dean Burgon felt that the TEXTUS RECEPTUS was a good text, and better by far than that either of Lachmann, Tregelles, Tischendorf, or Westcott and Hort. (2) Dean Dean Burgon felt that, though the TEXTUS RECEPTUS was an excellent text for use in the meantime, and a thousand times superior to the Westcott and Hort text, yet he did not hold to its perfection. (3) Dean Dean Burgon believed firmly in the vital importance of the Church Fathers' quotations of the New Testament for critical use in any future revision of the TEXTUS RECEPTUS. (4) Dean Dean Burgon gave specific suggestions and **WARNINGS** both as to "HOW" and "WHEN" he would make a major revision of the TEXTUS RECEPTUS (pp. 5-39).

3. Section three discussed Dean Dean Burgon's prerequisites and **WARNINGS** for any major revision of the English King James (Authorized) Bible under four major headings: (1) Dean Dean Burgon gave an assessment of the errors of the English Revised Version of 1881 (E.R.V.) as being hopelessly at fault. (2) Dean Dean Burgon held in high esteem the Authorized (King James) Bible of 1611, (3) Dean Dean Burgon gave some suggestions as to WHEN a major revision of the King James Bible should be made, and what things should PRECEDE such revision. (4) Dean Dean Burgon discussed some of the principles of translation which should prevail for any revision of the King James (Authorized) Bible (pp. 41-54).

4. Section four (the present section), offered some points of SUMMARY and some CONCLUSIONS (pp. 55-69).

B. Conclusions. Though not complete, the following are some of the more important conclusions that can be derived from the foregoing study:

1. Conclusions Regarding Dean Burgon and the Greek Text.

(1) Dean Burgon Had No Confidence Whatsoever in the Greek Texts Of Lachmann, Tregelles, Tischendorf, or Westcott and Hort. Some of the critical terms used by Dean Burgon to show his lack of confidence in the basic Greek Text which was shared by all of these editors are as follows:

> (a) It is a *"mischievous"* text (p. 13).
>
> (b) It is *"untrustworthy from beginningto end"* (p. 13).
>
> (c) It has been constructed throughout on an *"utterly erroneous hypothesis."* (p. 13).
>
> (d) It is a *"systematic depravation"* of the Greek text (p. 13).
>
> (e) It is a *"poisoning of the River of Life at its Sacred source"* (p. 13).
>
> (f) It has *"deliberately rejected the Words of inspiration in every page"* and *"substituted for them fabricated readings"* (p. 14).
>
> (g) It has made the *"Words of inspiration"* as *"seriously imperilled"* (p. 13-14).
>
> (h) It is *"the most depraved"* text (p. 14)
>
> (i) It is a *"text vastly more remote from the inspired autographs"* than *"any which has appeared since the invention of printing"* (p. 15).
>
> (j) It is filled with *"conjectural emendation"* which has no place in *"Biblical textual criticism."* (p. 15)
>
> (k) It has departed from the *"Traditional Text"* *"nearly 6,000 times"* and almost *"invariably for the worse"* (p. 15).
>
> (l) It is a *"text demonstrably more remote from the Evangelic verity, than any which has ever yet seen the light"* (p. 16).
>
> (m) It is *"the most vicious recension of the original Greek in existence"* (p. 16).
>
> (n) It is *"hopelessly depraved throughout."* (p. 16)
>
> (o) It is a *"thousand times worse"* than the text of

Erasmus, the Complutensian, Stephens, Beza, and the Elzevirs. (p. 16).

(p) It has been guilty of *"falsifying the inspired Greek text in countless places"* and also *"branding with suspicion some of the most precious utterances of the Spirit"* (p. 17).

(q) It manifests a *"weak superstition"* which is *"without proof of any kind"* based on an *"utterly depraved archetype"* which should be *"unconditionally abandoned."* (p. 17).

(r) It is a *"prodigious blunder"* and contains *"vile fabrications"* (p. 17)

(s) It has many *"patent and scandalous defects and blemishes"* (p. 18).

(t) It is based on *"two of the least trustworthy documents in existence."* (p. 19).

(u) It is *"by far the foulest text that has ever seen the light."* (p. 19).

(v) It is based upon a Greek text of *"essential rottenness"* (p. 20).

(2) Dean Burgon Had Great Confidence in the Traditional Greek Text (the Textus Receptus) as Being Fundamentally Sound. Some of the commendations Dean Burgon made concerning the Textus Receptus or Traditional Text of the Greek New Testament are as follows:

(a) Even its enemy, Hort, admitted the Textus Receptus was *"beyond all question the text of the second half of the fourth century."* (p. 8).

(b) Dean Burgon used various terms to designate the *"Textus Receptus,"* including *"the Traditional Greek text,"* the *"Erasmian"* text, the *"Complutensian,"* the *"text of Stephens"* or of *"Beza"* or of the *"Elzevirs"* or *"the Received"* text, or *"whatever name you please."* (p. 9).

(c) Dean Burgon said the Textus Receptus is a *"text which has cone down to us which is attested by a general consensus of ancient copies, ancient Fathers, ancient versions."* (p. 9).

(d) Dean Burgon agreed with Hort's *"viritual admission"* that *"beyond all question the Textus Receptus is the dominant Graeco-Syrian text of A.D. 350 to A.D. 400."* (p. 9)

(e) Dean Burgon said the Textus Receptus was *"identical with the text of every extant lectionary of the Greek Church"* (p.

10).

(f) Dean Burgon said the Textus Receptus *"cannot seriously be suspected of error"* (p. 10).

(g) Dean Burgon plead.for the Textus Receptus to be the *"standard whereby to test"* various manuscripts. *"To the end of time it will probably be the practice of scholars to compare MSS. of the New Testamentwith the Received Text."* (pp. 10-11).

(h) Dean Burgon said the Textus Receptus was the text which *"was universally employed throughout Europe for the first 300 years afte rthe invention of printing"* and *"practically identical with the text which was in popular use at the end of three centuries from the date of the Sacred autographs themselves: in other words, being more than 1500 years old"* (p. 11).

(i) Dean Burgon said that the *"Textus Receptus is not the first edition of Erasmus,"* but that *"first edition"* was merely *"the humblest ancestor of the Textus Receptus."* (p. 11).

(j) Dean Burgon defended the Erasmian manuscripts by saying that *"the manuscripts which Erasmus used differ, for the most part, only in small and insignificant details from the bulk of the cursive manuscripts. The general character of their text is the same. By this observation the pedigree of the Received Text is carried up beyond the individual manuscripts used by Erasmus . . . . that pedigree stretches back to a remote antiquity. **The first ancestor of the Received Text was at least contemporary with the oldest of our extant manuscripts, if not older than any of them.**"* (pp. 11-12).

(k) Dean Burgon held that *"the Complutensian, which was printed in 1514, exhibits the Traditional Text with the same general fidelity as the Erasmian, which did not see the light till two years later."* (p. 12).

(l) Dean Burgon said that, in his day (1883 A.D.), *"essentially the Received Text is full 1550 years old,--(yes, and a vast deal older),"* and that *"**I esteem it quite good enough for all ordinary purposes.**"* (p.12).

(3) Dean Burgon Did Not Hold to the "Perfection" of the Textus Receptus, But Agreed it Calls for "Revision" in Some Areas, But that "Revision" Must Be Based on Sound Principles Such as He Suggested, Rather than Those Used by Westcott and Hort. Some of Dean Burgon's statements on this theme are as follows:

(a) Dean Burgon did not hold *the "commonly Received*

text" as *"the final standard of appeal"* but only as a good *"common standard"* for comparison of texts, rather than *"the absolute standard of excellence."* (p. 22).

(b) Dean Burgon felt that *"in not a few particulars, the 'Textus Receptus' does call for revision, certainly; although revision on entirely different principles from those which were found to have prevailed in the Jerusalem Chamber"* [of the E.R.V. using Westcott and Hort's text] (p. 22).

(c) Though Dean Burgon held that *"from a variety of sources"* the Textus Receptus is *"essentially the same in all"* sources, yet *"it requires revision in respect of many of its lesser details."* (p. 22).

(d) Dean Burgon spoke highly, however, of the *"Textus Receptus"* as being ***"an excellent text as it stands, and that the use of it will never lead critical students of Scripture seriously astray.*** *--which is what no one will venture to predicate concerning any single critical edition of the N.T. which has been published since the days of Griesbach, by the disciples of Griesbach's school"* (p. 23).

(e) Dean Burgon did not take *"the Received"* text, or *"any other known text"* as *"a standard from which there shall be no appeal."* (p. 23).

(f) Though Dean Burgon felt the *"Received Text"* was *"full 1550 years old"* and *"a vast deal older,"* and he esteemed it *"quite good enough for all ordinary purposes,"* yet he *"eagerly makes"* his *"appeal from it to the threefold witness of copies, versions, Fathers, whenever"* he finds *"its testimony challenged."* (p. 24).

(4) Dean Burgon Demanded the Use of the "Church Fathers" for any Proposed "Revision" of the "Textus Receptus" in Addition to Use of "Lectionaries," "Versions," and "Copies."

Dean Burgon's statements can be summarized as follows on this point

(a) Dean Burgon rebuked Hort for *"getting rid of the testimony of the whole body of the Fathers"* and not receiving *"clear and consentient Patristic testimony to the text of Scripture"* as *"forcible witness to its truth."* (p. 25).

(b) Dean Burgon held that when the *"Church Fathers"* would *"witness to the reading of their own copies, their testimony on the point, to say the least, is worthy of the most respectful attention. Dated codices, in fact are they, to all intents and purposes, as often as they bear clear witness to the text of Scripture."* (p. 25).

(c) Dean Burgon believed that *"every attesting Father*

is perceived to be a dated MS. and an independent authority; and the combined evidence of several of these becomes simply unmanageable." (p. 26).

(d) Dean Burgon, in rebuking Westcott and Hort's failure to use the Church Fathers' testimony in arriving at the true text of Scripture, felt that these Fathers, where clear, were *"dated manuscripts,"* *"authentic utterances of famous doctors and Fathers of the church,"* *"sure witnesses of what was accounted Scripture in a known region, by a famous personage, at a well-ascertained period."* (p. 26).

(5) Dean Burgon Had Some Specific Suggestions Both as to "How" and "When" a "Major Revision" of the Textus Receptus Should Be Undertaken Following Meticulously His Sound Approach to Textual Criticism. Some of Dean Burgon's suggestions are summarized as follows:

(a). Dean Burgon stated that textual criticism as a subject was *"a very intricate one and abounds in unexplored problems"* (p. 27).

(b) Dean Burgon said that textual criticism demands a person's *"undivided attention for an extended period,"* in fact, he felt *"for many years past"* a man should give to textual criticism the *"whole of his time"* and *"sacrificed health, ease, relaxation, even necessary rest, to this one object"* and should make it *"his one business to aquire such an independent mastery of the subject as shall qualify him to do battle successfully for the imperilled letter of God's Word."* (p. 27).

(c) Dean Burgon advocated a *"laborious"* and a *"scientific method"* where a *"long summer day disappears"* quickly, and an entire week goes by with only *"a page of illegible manuscript"* *"to show for a week's heavy toil"* yet this is *"the indispensable condition of progress in an unexplored region, that a few should thus labour, until a path has been cut through the forest."* (p. 28).

(d) Dean Burgon's *"method"* which he *"advocates in every case of a supposed doubtful reading"* is that *"an appeal shall be unreservedly made to catholic antiquity; and that the combined verdict of manuscripts, versions, Fathers, shall be regarded as decisive."* (p. 28).

(e) Dean Burgon held that using this laborious method of inquiry *"would result in gradual accesssions of certain knowledge. After many years it might be found practicable to put forth by authority a carefully considered revision of the conmonly Received Greek text."* (p. 29).

(f) Dean Burgon described more completely his appeal

in textual criticism to the *"vast multitude of copies,"* the *"versions,"* the *"Fathers"* and the *"Lectionaries"* (p. 29).

(g) Dean Burgon *"resolutely maintained"* that *"external evidence must after all be our best, our only safe guide"* (p. 31).

(h) Dean Burgon's critical method in *"every case of doubt or difficulty--supposed or real"* must *"be the same: namely, after patiently collecting all the available evidence, then, without partiality or prejudice, to adjudicate between the conflicting authorities, and loyally to accept that verdict for which there is clearly the preponderating evidence."* (p. 31).

(i) Dean Burgon cautioned, however, that *"__nothing may be rejected from the commonly Received Text, except on evidence which shall clearly outweigh the evidence for retaining it.__"* (p. 31).

(j) Dean Burgon also stated that *"__whenever the evidence is about evenly balanced, few it is hoped will deny that the text which has been 'in possession' for three centuries and a half, and which rests on infinitely better manuscript evidence than that of any ancient work which can be named,--should, for every reason, be let alone__"* (p. 32).

(k) Dean Burgon stressed use of *"external evidence"* and *"never from postulates of the imagination"* should a text be established. (p. 32).

(l) Dean Burgon said *"we begrudge no amount of labour: reckoning a long summer's day well spent if it has enabled us to ascertain the truth concerning one single controverted Word of Scripture."* (p. 32).

(m) Dean Burgon evidenced his own scepticism and conservatism on textual revision when he wrote that *"exactly eight"* of the E.R.V. committee of 1881 would have been able to revise correctly the Greek text of the New Testament provided they were:

(1) *"divines of undoubted orthodoxy"*
(2) of *"splendid scholarship"*
(3) of *"proficiency of the best learning"*
(4) and then only they *"might"* succeed;
(5) *"under certain safeguards"*
(6) could the work be *"safely entrusted"* to them;
(7) *"under the guidance of Prebendary Scrivener"*
(8) but only *"when unanimous"* in their decisions;
(9) could they have *"materially erred"*
(10) provided that each had had a *"previous"* and
(11) *"life-long familiarity with the science of textual*

criticism"

(12) or *"at least leisure for prosecuting it now, for ten or twenty years,"*

(13) with *"absolutely undivided attention"* as an indispensable requisite for the success of such an undertaking" and

(14) this *"undeniable, is a qualification rather to be desiderated* [that is, "desired"] *than looked for at the hands of English divines of note in our present day."* (pp. 32-33).

What Dean Burgon was saying in the above conditions was that even in his day, they were by no means ready for a proper revision of the Received Text.

(n) Dean Burgon stated that for "an authoritative revision of the Greek text" the *"time has not yet come"* even in 1883. He agreed in this with Ellicott who said, *"for any authoritative revision, we are not yet mature: either in Biblical learning or Hellenistic scholarship"* (p. 34).

(o) Dean Burgon said that though he had access to *"more manuscripts than were available when the Textus Receptus was formed,"* yet *"who knows how to use them?"* (p. 34).

(p) Dean Burgon said though more *"ancient versions"* were available, yet *"what living Englishman* [then in 1883] *is able to tell us what they all contain? A smattering acquaintance with the langauges of ancient Egypt,--the Gothic, Aethiopic, Armenian, Georgian and Slavonian versions,--is of no manner of avail."* (p. 35).

(q) Dean Burgon said though *"the Fathers have been better edited"* yet *"which of the Fathers has been satisfactorily indexed?"* (p. 36).

(r) Dean Burgon called for an entire *"generation of students"* to *"give themselves entirely up to this neglected branch of sacred science"* (i.e. textual criticism). (p. 36).

(s) Dean Burgon called for *"at least 500 more copies"* of the New Testament to *"be diligently collated"* (p. 36).

(t) Dean Burgon called for *"at least 100 of the ancient Lectionaries"* to *"be very exactly collated."* (p. 36).

(u) Dean Burgon called for *"the most important of the ancient versions"* to be *"edited afresh"* and *"let the languages in which these are written be for the first time really mastered by Englishmen"* (p. 37).

(v) Dean Burgon called for *"the Fathers"* to be

"ransacked and indexed" to *"give up their precious secrets"* to know the *"evidence which they afford"* (p. 37).

(w) Dean Burgon did not believe we could *"obtain a Greek text on which absolute reliance may be placed"* unless the preceding many safeguards were <u>all</u> completed. (p. 37).

(x) Dean Burgon called for the *"printing"* of any *"unpublished works of the ancient Greek Fathers"* which are *"anywhere known to exist"* (pp. 37-38).

(y) Dean Burgon felt that *"the science of textual criticism will have to be prosecuted, for the first time, in a scholarlike manner."* (p. 38).

(z) Dean Burgon said that the *"principles"* of Westcott and Hort, and their followers, for establishing a sound Greek text *"cannot be too soon or too unconditionally abandoned"* (p. 38)

(a') Dean Burgon insisted on the *"only trustworthy method"* of *"ascertaining the truth of Scripture"* must be the *"method which, without prejudice or partiality,--simply ascertains which form of the text enjoys the earliest, the fullest, the widest, and most respectable, and--above all things--the most varied attestation."* (p. 39)

(b') Dean Burgon insisted that the textual critic must have a *"clear head and a calm, dispassionate judgment"* (p. 39).

(c') Dean Burgon held that *"no compomise is possible"* between *"the new German system"* of Westcott and Hort and others, and the *"old English school"* of textual criticism which Dean Burgon followed, because they are *"antagonistic throughout"* and have *"nothing in common"* (p. 40).

(d') Dean Burgon insisted that *"the truth of the text of Scripture is to be elicited exclusively from the consentient testimony of the largest number of the best copies, Fathers, versions."* (p. 40).

(e') Dean Burgon suggested three *"convenient test places"* between the opposing textual schools: *"The Last Twelve Verses of S. Mark's Gospel"*; *"the angelic hymn"* (Luke 2:14); and *"1 Timothy 3:16"* (p. 41).

2.   Conclusions Regarding Dean Burgon and the English King James (Authorized) Bible Text.

(1) Dean Burgon Had No Confidence Whatsoever in the English Revised Version (E.R.V.) of 1881. Some of the descriptions and assessments of the English Revised Version (E.R.V.) of 1881 made by Dean Burgon are as follows:

(a) It is *"hopelessly at fault"* (p. 42).

(b) It is a *"very unsatisfactory product. Their uncouth phraseology and their jerky sentences, their pedantic obscurity and their unidiomatic English, contrast painfully with the 'happy turns of expression, the music of the cadences, the felicities of the rhythm' of our Authorized Bible"* (p. 43).

(c) In the *E.R.V. "our Authorized English Version has been silently revised"* (p. 43).

(d) It is an *"unfortunate production"* and *"the old is better"* (p. 44).

(e) Dean Burgon stated *"their work is disfigured throughout by changes which convict a majority of their body alike of an imperfect acquaintance with the genius of the Greek language, and of scarcely a moderate appreciation of the idiomatic properties of their own"* (p. 45).

(f) It is a *"schoolboy method of translation"* and *"oppressive"* (p. 45).

(g) Its errors are twofold:

"(1) to exhibit a singular indifference to the properties of English speech, while they maintain a servile adherence (etymological or idiomatic, as the case may be) to the Greek:--

(2) Right or wrong, to part company from William Tyndale and the giants who gave us our 'Authorized Version'" (p. 45).

(h) It exhibited a *"spirit of servile pedantry"* and *"the atmosphere of the lecture-room"* (p. 45).

(i) It followed the *"mistaken principle"* of *"translating, as far as possible, the same Greek word by the same English word"* (p. 46).

(j) It contained *"queer uncouth phraseology," "jerky sentences," "pedantic obscurity,"* a *"stiff, constrained manner,"* a *"fidgetty affectation of accuracy,"* a *"habitual achievement of English which fails to exhibit the spirit of the original Greek,"* an *"unreadable"* work, and a *"hopeless"* translation (p. 47).

(k) It should be *"ploughed up--ploughed deep"* (p. 48).

(l) It exhibits *"tasteless, injudicious, and unsatisfactory essays in translation"* (p. 48).

(m) It is *"for the most part,"* a *"first-rate school-boy's crib,--tasteless, unlovely, harsh, unidiomatic,--servile without being really faithful,--pedantic without being really learned;--an unreadable translation, in short; the result of a vast amount of labour indeed, but of wondrous little skill"* (p. 48).

(n) It contains *"changes, which are vexations, teasing, and irritating"* (p. 49).

(2) Dean Burgon had high praise for the excellence of the King James (Authorized) Bible. Some of Dean Burgon's comments on the excellence of the King James Bible are summarized as follows:

(a) Dean Burgon described the New Testament as having *"happy turns of expression, the music of the cadences, the felicities of the rhythm"* like a *"well-built carriage"* (p. 43).

(b) Dean Burgon believed a *"revision"* of the A.V. involved a *"tremendous risk"* because *"our Authorized Version is the one religious link which at present binds together ninety millions of English-speaking men scattered over the earth's surface"* (p. 49).

(c) Dean Burgon said that *"no 'revision' of our authorized version, however judiciously executed, will ever occupy the place in public esteem which is actually enjoyed by the work of the translators of 1611,--the noblest literary work in the Anglo-Saxon language"* (pp. 49-50).

(d) Dean Burgon said *"the men of 1611--above all that William Tyndale 77 years before them--produced a work of real genius"* (p. 50)

(e) Dean Burgon felt that the *"translators of 1611"* were men who *"understood their craft. 'There were giants in those days.'"* because *"the Spirit of their God was mightily upon them"* (p. 51).

(f) Dean Burgon described the New Testament as *"a noble version,"* with *"dignified simplicity and essential faithfulness,"* and *"manly grace"* and *"delightful rhythm"* with *"living freshness, and elastic freedom, and habitual fidelity"* (p. 51).

(g) Dean Burgon called the New Testament a *"priceless treasure"* bequeathed to us *"by the piety and wisdom of our fathers"* (p. 51).

(h) Dean Burgon stated: *"how very seldom our Authorized Version is materially wrong; how faithful and trustworthy, on the contrary, it is throughout"* (p. 51).

(3) Dean Burgon Had Some Specific Suggestions Both as to "How" and "When" a "Major Revision" of the King James (Authorized) Bible of the English New Testament Should Be Undertaken. Some of Dean Burgon's suggestions are summarized as follows:

(a) Dean Burgon insisted that *"an authoritative*

revision of the Greek text will have to precede any future revision of the English of the New Testament" (p. 52).

(b) Dean Burgon said *"partisanship must be completely outlived,--before the church can venture, with the remotest prospect of a successful issue, to organize another attempt at revising the Authorized Version of the New Testament Scriptures"* and that *"time must be given for passion and prejudice to cool effectually down"* (p. 53).

(4) Dean Burgon Had Some Specific Suggestions as to "Principles of Translation Which Should Prevail in any Future "Major Revision" of the King James (Authorized) Bible. Some of Dean Burgon's principles on this point are summarized as follows:

(a) Any *"revision"* of the New Testament would only be as a *"companion in the study"* and *"for private edification"* and as a *"book of reference for critical purposes, especially in respect of difficult and controverted passages"* but not for public use. (pp. 53-54).

(b) Dean Burgon said a *"revised edition"* of the A.V. *"if executed with consummate ability and learning"* would be *"a work of inestimable value"* (p. 54).

(c) Dean Burgon suggested a *"revision"* of the New Testament *"by marginal notes or in some other way"* which he did not determine at that point (p. 54).

(d) Dean Burgon held any *"revision"* of the King James Bible to be only *"as a handmaid"* to the King James Bible, but he was *"thoroughly convinced"* that such *"revision"* should not be *"intended to supersede"* the New Testament. He felt *"a rival translation is not to be entertained for a moment"* and he *"deprecated"* such a *"rival translation"* *"entirely"* (p. 54).

(e) Dean Burgon felt that where the *"laws of English idiom"* and the *"laws of Greek grammar"* might *"clash in what is meant to be a translation into English out of Greek,"* the *"Greek grammar"* laws must *"give way"* to the *"laws of English idiom"* (p. 54).

(f) Dean Burgon believed that *"the phenomena of language are among the most subtle and delicate imaginable: the problem of translation, one of the most manysided and difficult that can be named. And if this holds universally, in how much greater a degree when the book to be translated is the Bible."* (p. 55).

3. Conclusions Making Use of Dean Burgon's Conclusions on the Textus Receptus and the King James (Authorized) Bible for Today's Textual and

Translation Problems. Though Dean Burgon's conclusions were limited to his own day (1813-1888 A.D.), yet there are certain conclusions which can be extrapolated from his own and be up-dated and brought to bear on the various problems of our own day. It would therefore be helpful to outline a few of such conclusions in this section:

(1) **Dean Burgon, if alive today**, would have no confidence in the modern Greek critical New Testament texts of Souter, Nestle, United Bible Society, Aland, or others since they're based essentially on the same erroneously-based text as Westcott and Hort's.

(2) **Dean Burgon, if alive today,** would continue to have confidence in the Textus Receptus until and unless satisfactory major revision were made based upon his principles.

(3) **Dean Burgon, if alive today,** would still have insisted on the great importance of the Church Fathers' quotations of the New Testament in any revision attempt.

(4) **Dean Burgon, if alive today,** would continue to have confidence in the superiority of the King James (Authorized) Bible until and unless the Greek textual basis is revised according to Dean Burgon's principles.

(5) **Dean Burgon, if alive today,** would not be in favor of using any revision of the King James Bible in public worship as a *"rival translation,"* but only privately and in the study.

(6) **Dean Burgon, if alive today,** would favor a method of *"revision"* of the King James Bible making use of *"marginal notes"* which would explain any difficult words in the text, or any other difficulties which might seem to be there.

(7) **Dean Burgon, if alive today,** would not favor any of the New Testament English translations such as N.E.V., N.I.V., L.B., T.E.V., N.A.S.V., etc., because of their deficiencies similar to those he specified for the E.R.V. of 1881.

(8) **Dean Burgon, if alive today,** would not favor any of the New Testament English translations mentioned above, and others of similar nature, because they are based upon the false and erroneous Westcott and Hort Greek text with minor modifications.

(9) **Dean Burgon, if alive aoday,** would still believe the *"time has not yet come"* for a major revision of the Textus Receptus for the following reasons:

(a) **The Necessary Ground Work in Preparing the Materials for Major Revision Has Not Yet Been Done.**

(1) The Church Fathers have not as yet been better edited, and an INDEX to the entire Fathers' quotations of Scripture has not been published (though Dean Burgon's INDEX in the British Museum is an excellent beginning on this project).

(2) The unpublished works of various Church Fathers have not as yet been published.

(3) At least 500 more copies of the New Testament in Greek have not as yet been *"diligently collated."*

(4) at least 100 of the ancient Lectionaries have not as yet been *"very exactly collated."*

(5) the most important of the ancient versions have not been *"edited afresh."*

(b) The Necessary Ground Work in Preparing the Personnel for Major Revision Has not yet Been Done.

I' There Is not yet a Sufficient Number of Workers in Textual Criticism Who are Thoroughly Committed to Dean Burgon's Sound Principles. For example:

(1) There are not enough who have rejected the false methodology of Westcott and Hort, and are thoroughly committed to Dean Burgon's sound methods in this important field.

(2) There are not enough who agree with Dean Burgon that this field is *"a very intricate one"* which *"abounds in unexplored problems."*

(3) There are not enough who have given *"undivided attention for an extended period"* to this field *"for many years past."*

(4) There are not enough who have given and will give the *"whole"* of their *"time"* and who *will* "sacrifice health, ease, relaxation, even necessary rest" for this cause.

(5) There are not enough who will shoulder the *"laborious"* task of such a *"scientific method"* as Dean Burgon proposed for this field.

(6) There are not enough who have qualified for the task with *"proficiency of the best learning"* in this field.

(7) There are not enough who have followed Burgon's methodology and deep, protracted study for at least *"ten or twenty years"* with *"absolutely undivided attention"* as an *"indispensable requisite for the success of such an undertaking."*

II' There Is Not Yet a Sufficient Quality of Workers in Textual Criticism Who Are Thoroughly Committed to Dean Burgon's Sound Principles Including Their Sound Academic Preparations for Such a Monumental Task. For example:

(1) There are not yet sufficient numbers of Dean Burgonian Textual Critics who know how to make use of all the materials represented in the copies of the Greek New Testament.

(2) There are not yet sufficient numbers of Dean Burgonian textual critics who are able to tell us what the *"ancient Versions"* contain. This would necessitate more than a *"smattering acquaintance"* with the *"languages of ancient Egypt,--the Gothic, Aethiopic, Armenian, Georgian and Slavonian versions."* These languages *"must be mastered by Englishmen"* and Americans before they can be effectively used in this great task.

APPENDIX I
THE LINGUISTIC TRAINING
AND QUALIFICATIONS OF
SOME OF THE TRANSLATORS OF
THE KING JAMES BIBLE OF 1611

There is a great decrease in genuine scholarship in our modern times. This has been true for many years. Compared to the soundness of academic preparation and learning in the days of the King James (Authorized) Bible of 1611, even in Dean John William Burgon's day (1813-1888 A.D.)-- though much better than in our present day--genuine scholarship had begun to disintegrate.

To illustrate this, it would be well to highlight some of the qualifications of a few of the translators of the King James Bible. Dean Burgon, in looking over the English landscape in his own day, was not able to find.a sufficient number of men who were in all respects fully qualified by background, training, and temperament, to make a major revision of the Textus Receptus. How much less are we able to find them today.

I. The Linguistic Qualifications of William Tyndale Whose Translation (77 Years Before the KJB) Was Used Extensively by the KJB Translators.

The main source of information in this section is *The Translators Revived: A Biographical Memoir of the Authors of the English Version of the Holy Bible* by Alexander W. McClure, D.D. It was written in about 1857 and has about 250 pages. It can be secured as **B.F.T. #1419 @ $13.00**. It mentions Tyndale and his *"high learning in Hebrew, Greek and Latin."* (McClure, *Translators Revived,* p. 27). He, in fact, was *"so skilled in the seven languages, Hebrew, Greek, Latin, Italian, Spanish, English, and French, that whichever he spake, you would suppose it his native tongue."* (McClure, *Translators Revived*, pp. 27-28).

II. The Linguistic Qualifications of Some of the King James Bible Translators.

From *TheTranslators Revived*, as mentioned above, the following facts were secured on some of the translators of our King James Bible of

1611.

A. From Company #1–The Westminster Group (Books of Moses and Historical Books Through the End of 2nd Kings)

1. Lancelot Andrews. He *"acquired most of the modern languages of Europe. At the University* [Univ. of Cambridge, that is], *he gave himself chiefly to the Oriental tongues and to divinity."* (McClure, *Translators Revived*, p. 78). Lancelot Andrews' *"manual for his private devotions, prepared by himself, is wholly in the Greek language."* (McClure, *Translators Revived*, p. 86).

Such was his skill in all languages, especially the Oriental, that, had he been present at the confusion of tongues at Babel, he might have served as interpreter-general! In his funeral sermon by Dr. Buckeridge, Bishop of Rochester, it is said that Dr. Andrews was conversant with fifteen languages. (McClure, *Translators Revived*, p. 87.)

2. John Overall. He was *"celebrated for the appropriateness of his quotations from the Fathers"* (McClure, *Translators Revived*, p. 89).

He had spoken Latin so long, it was troublesome to him to speak English in a continued oration. . . . Though long familiarity with other languages may have made him somewhat inapt for continuous public discourse in his mother-tongue, he was thereby the better fitted to discern the sense of the Sacred Original. (McClure, *Translators Revived*, pp. 89-90, 91).

3. Hadrian Saravia. Saravia published several Latin treatises against Beza, Danaeus, and other Presbyterians . . . . [he was] educated in all kinds of literature in his younger days, especially in several languages . . . . in particular the Arch-prelate relied much on Dr. Saravia's Hebrew learning in his contests with Hugh Broughton. (McClure, *Translators Revived*, pp. 94, 95).

4. Robert Tighe. He was characterized as *"an excellent textuary and profound linguist."* (McClure, *Translators Revived*, p. 98).

5. Geoffry King. McClure wrote of him:

Mr. King was fellow of King's College, Cambridge. It is a fair token of his fitness to take part in this translation-work, that he succeeded Mr. Spaulding, another of these translators, as Regius Professor of Hebrew in that University. Men were not appointed in those days to such duties of instruction, with the expectation that they would qualify themselves after their induction into office. (McClure, *Translators Revived*, p. 99).

6.   William Bedwell. Bedwell was justly reputed to have been "an eminent oriental scholar." He published in quarto an edition of the Epistles of St. John in Arabic, with a Latin version, printed at the press of Raphel Engius, at Antwerp, in 1612.

He also left many arabic manuscripts to the University of Cambridge, with numerous notes upon them, and a font of types for printing them. His fame for Arabic learning was so great, that when Erpenius, a most renowned orientalist, resided in England, in 1606, he was much indebted to Bedwell for direction in his studies. To Bedwell, rather than to Erpenius, who commonly enjoys it, belongs the honor of being the first who considerably promoted and revived the study of the Arabic language and literature in Europe. He was also tutor to another Orientalist of renown, Dr. Pococke. For many years, Mr. Bedwell was engaged in preparing an Arabic lexicon in three volumes. (McClure, *Translators Revived*, pp. 100-01).

After Bedwell's death, the voluminous manuscripts of his lexicon were loaned by the University of Cambridge to aid in the compilation of Dr. Castell's colossal work, the *Lexicon Heptaglotton*. Some modern scholars have fancied that we have an advantage in our times [i.e. c. 1857 when this book was written by McClure] over the translators of the King James's day, by reason of the greater attention which is supposed to be paid at present to what are called the "cognate" and "Shemitic" languages, and especially the Arabic by which much light is thought to be reflected upon Hebrew words and phrases. It is evident, however, that Mr. Bedwell and others, among his fellow-laborers, were thoroughly conversant in this part of the broad field of sacred criticism. Mr. Bedwell also commenced a Persian dictionary, which is among Archbishop Laud's manuscripts, still preserved in the Bodleian Library at Oxford. (McClure, *Translators Revived*, pp. 101-02).

B.   From   Company   #2--The   Cambridge   Group (Books of 1 Chronicles Through the End of the Song of Solomon).

1.   Edward Lively. He was King's Professor of Hebrew" at Trinity College, Cambridge University . . . Much dependence was placed on his surpassing skill in the Oriental tongues . . . . he was author of a Latin exposition of five of the minor prophets, and a work on chronology. Dr. Pusey, of Oxford, says that Lively, 'whom Pockocke never mentions but with great respect, was probably, next to Pockocke, the greatest of our Hebraists.' (McClure, *Translators Revived*, pp. 103-4).

    2.   John Richardson. He was *"a most excellent linguist"* and held *"public disputes in the Latin tongue"* as a regular occurrence. McClure,.*Translators Revived*, p. 105).

    3.   Lawrence Chaderton. McClure wrote of him:
He made himself familiar with the Latin, Greek, and Hebrew tongues, and was thoroughly skilled in them. . . . His studies were such as eminently qualify him to bear an important part in the translating of the Bible. . . . He was a scholar, and a ripe and good one. Having reached his threescore years and ten, his knowledge was fully digested, and his experience matured . . . but where shall we find men for the work like those who gave us our version of the Bible? (McClure, *Translators Revived*, pp. 108-9, 112-13, 116).

    4.   Francis Dillingham. He often took part in *"A Greek act"* which was a
"debate carried on in the Greek tongue." He was not without reason styled the "great Grecian." He was noted as an excellent linguist and a subtle disputant. . . . He published a manual of the Christian Faith, taken from the Fathers. (McClure, *Translators Revived*, pp. 116-17).

    5.   Roger Andrews. *"He too was a famous linguist in his time, like his brother Lancelot, the Bishop of Winchester."* (McClure, *Translators Revived*, pp. 117-18).

    6.   Thomas Harrison. McClure wrote of him:
On account of his exquisite skill in the Hebrew and Greek idioms, he was one of the chief examiners in the University [i.e. Trinity College, Cambridge University] of those who sought to be public professors of these languages. (McClure, *Translators Revived*, p. 118).

    7.   Robert Spaulding. McClure wrote of him:
Dr. Spauldtng was fellow of St. John's College, Cambridge. He succeeded Edward Lively, of whom we have briefly spoken, as Regius Professor of Hebrew. (McClure, *Translators Revived*, p. 119).

8.   Andrew Bing. McClure wrote of him:

In course of time he succeeded Geoffry King who was Dr. Spaulding's successor, in the Regius Professorship in Hebrew. (McClure, *Translators Revived*, p. 119).

C.   From Company #3—The Oxford Group (Books of Isaiah Through the End of the Old Testament Book of Malachi).

1.   John Harding. McClure wrote of him:

He had been Royal Professor of Hebrew in the University [i.e. Oxford University] for thirteen years. . . . the share which he, with his brethren, performed, was, perhaps, the most difficult portion of the translation work. (McClure, *Translators Revived*, pp. 120-21).

2.   John Reynolds. McClure wrote of him:

He became a fellow in 1566, at the early age of seventeen [i.e. at Corpus Christi College]. Six years later he was made Greek lecturer in his College, . . . determined to explore the whole field, and make himself master of the subject, he devoted himself to the study of the Scriptures in the original tongues, and read all the Greek and Latin Fathers, and all the ancient records of the church. . . . the next year Dr. Reynolds was put upon the list of translators, on account of his well known skill in the Hebrew and Greek. . . . [he was] most excellent in all tongues useful or ornamental to a divine. . . . Nothing can tend more to inspire confidence in their version than the knowledge of their immense acquirements, almost incredible to the superficial scholars in this age of smatterers, sciolists, and pretenders [that is, in 1857]. [McClure, *Translators Revived*, pp. 121-22, 131-32, 133).

3.   Thomas Holland. McClure wrote of him:

He had a wonderful knowledge of all the learned languages, and of all arts and sciences, both human and divine. He was mighty in the Scriptures; and so familiarly acquainted with the Fathers, as if he himself had been one of them; . . . (McClure, *Translators Revived*, pp. 136-37).

4.   Richard Kilby. McClure wrote of him:

He was considered so accurate in Hebrew studies, that he was appointed the King's Professor in that branch of literature [i.e. at Oxford University] . . . . Dr. Kilby was a man of so great learning and wisdom, and so excellent a critic in the Hebrew tongue, that he was made professor of it in this university [Oxford]; and was also so perfect a Grecian, that he was by King James appointed to be one of the translators of the Bible; . . . (McClure, *Translators Revived*, pp. 138-39).

5.   Miles Smith. McClure wrote of him:
He had a four-fold share in the translation [1] he not only served in the third company, but [2] was one of the twelve selected to revise the work, after which it was referred to the final examination [3] of Dr. Smith and Bishop Bilson. [4] last of all, Dr. Smith was employed to write that most learned and eloquent preface. . . . He went through the Greek and Latin Fathers, making his annotations on them all. He was well acquainted with the Rabbinacal glosses and comments. So expert was he in the Chaldee, Syriac, and Arabic, that they were almost as familiar as his native tongue. 'Hebrew he had at his fingers' ends' . . . (McClure, *Translators Revived*, pp. 142-43)

6.   Richard Brett. McClure wrote of him:
He was skilled and versed to a criticism in the Latin, Greek, Hebrew, Chaldee, Arabic, and Ethiopic tongues. He published a number of erudite works, all in Latin. (McClure, *Translators Revived*, p. 144).

D.   From Company #4—The Oxford Group (The Four Gospels, Acts, and Revelation).
1.   George Abbot. In 1598, Dr. Abbot published a Latin work which was reprinted in Germany. (McClure, *Translators Revived*, p. 153).

2.   Henry Savile. McClure wrote of him:
He became famous for his Greek and mathematical learning. . . In his twenty-ninth year, he travelled in France and elsewhere, to perfect himself in literature: and returned accomplished in learning, languages, and knowledge of the world and men. He then became tutor in Greek and mathematics to Queen Elizabeth. . . . He translated the *Histories of Cornelius Tacitus*, and published the same with notes. He also published, from the manuscripts, *The Writings of Bradwardin Against Pelagius; The Writers of English History Subsequent to Bede; Prelections on the Elements of Euclid*; and other learned works in English and Latin. He is chiefly known, however, by being the first to edit *The Complete Works of John Chrysostom*, the most famous of the Greek Fathers. . . . His edition of one thousand copies was published in 1613, and makes eight immense folios. . . . Sir

Henry Savile was one of the most profound, exact, and critical scholars of his age; and meet and ripe to take a prominent part in the preparation of our incomparable version. (McClure, *op. cit.*, pp. 164-65, 166-67, 169).

    3.   **John Peryn.** *"He was the Kings Professor of Greek in the University* [that is, Oxford University]*."* (McClure, *Translators Revived*, p. 170.)

    4.   **John Harmar.** McClure wrote of him:

He was appointed the King's Professor of Greek in 1585. He stood high in the crowd of tall scholars, the literary giants of the time. He published several learned works; among them, Latin translations of several of Chrysostom's writings, . . . the master of an excellent English style, and adept in the difficult art of translating. . . . He was a most noted Latinist, Grecian, and divine. . . . He was always accounted a most solid theologist, admirably well read in the Fathers and Schoolmen. . . . (McClure, *Translators Revived*, pp. 171-72).

  E.   **From Company #5–The Westminster Company (The New Testament Epistles).**

    1.   **John Spencer.** McClure wrote of him:

He was elected Greek lecturer for that college [i.e. Corpus Christi College, Oxford University] being then but nineteen years of age. . . . of his eminent scholarship there can be no question. He was a valuable helper in the great work of preparing our common English Version. (McClure, *Translators Revived*, pp. 177, 180).

    2.   **William Dakins**. McClure wrote of him:

He became Bachelor in Divinity in 1601. The next year he was appointed Greek lecturer. [i.e. at Trinity College, Cambridge University]. . . . he was considered peculiarly fit to be employed in this work, on account of his skill in the original languages. (McClure, *Translators Revived*, pp. 183-84).

  F.   **From Company #6–The Cambridge Group (All the Books of the Apocrypha).** [NOTE: There are seven reasons given on pages 185-186, as to why the apocryphal books were not admitted to the Canon of Scripture. It was made clear that the New Testament Translators *"by no means placed"* the Apocrypha *"on a level with the canonical books of Scripture."* (McClure, *Translators Revived*, p. 185.)]

    1.   **John Duport**. He was "a disguised Greek professor and divine." (McClure, *Translators Revived*, p. 189).

2.   Samuel Ward. He was *"so skilled in tongues . ."* (McClure, *op. cit*, p. 197).

3.   Andrew Downes. McClure wrote of him:
For full forty years he was Regius Professor of Greek in that famous university [i.e. St. John's College, Cambridge University] . . . . this venerable professor is spoken of as "one composed of Greek and industry." (McClure, *Translators Revived*, p. 198.)

4.   John Bois. McClure wrote of him:
"He was carefully taught by his father; and at the age of five years he had read the Bible **in Hebrew**. By the time he was six years old, he not only wrote Hebrew legibly, but in a fair and elegant character. (p. 200) . . . He soon distinguished himself by his great skill in Greek, writing letters in that language to the master and senior fellows. (p. 200) . . . He [Bois] there [in Dr. Downes' Chambers, who was the chief lecturer in the Greek language] read with him twelve Greek authors, in verse and prose, the hardest that could be found, both for dialect and phrase. It was a common practice with the young enthusiast to go to the University library at four o'clock in the morning, and stay without intermission till eight in the evening . (p. 201) . . . For ten years, he was Greek lecturer in his college [St. John's College, Cambridge University]; and during that time, he voluntarily lectured, in his own chamber, at four o'clock in the morning, most of the fellows being in attendance! It may be doubted, whether, at the present day [i.e. 1857], a teacher and class so zealous could be found at old Cambridge, new Cambridge, or anywhere else,--not excluding laborious Germany. (p. 201) . . . [his library] contained one of the most complete and costly collections of Greek literature that had ever been made. (p. 203) . . . in his translation of the Bible, he had a double share. After the completion of the Apocrypha, the portion assigned to his company, the other Cambridge company, to whom was assigned from the Chronicles to the Canticles inclusively, earnestly intreated his assistance, as he was equally distinguished for his skill in Greek and Hebrew. (p. 204) . . . During the four years thus employed, Mr. Bois gave close attention to the duty, from Monday morning to Saturday evening, spending the Sabbaths only at his rectory with his family. (p. 204) . . . When the work had been carried through the first stage, he was one of the twelve delegates sent two from each of the companies, to make the final revision of the

work at Stationers' Hall, in London. This occupied nine months,
. . . Mr. Bois took notes of all the proceedings of this
committee. (p. 204) . . . He left, at his death, as many leaves of
manuscript as he had lived days in his long life; for even in his
old age, he spent eight hours in daily study, mostly reading and
correcting ancient authors. Among his writings, was a voluminous commentary in Latin on the Gospels and Acts, which
was published some twelve years after his decease. (p. 205) He
was in the highest esteem with studious foreigners, and second
to none in solid attainments in the Greek tongue. He was so
familiar with the Greek Testament that he could, at any time,
turn to any word that it contained. (McClure, *Translators
Revived,* pp. 200-207).

**G.   Additional Men Who Helped the KJB Translation
But Not Assigned to Any Particular Company So Far as
the Records Are Concerned.**
    1.   John Aglionby. McClure wrote of him:
Dr. Aglionby was deeply read in the Fathers and the Schoolmen,
'an excellent linguist.' (McClure, *Translators Revived*, p. 210).
    2.   Leonard Hutten. McClure wrote of him:
He was well known as an "excellent Grecian," and an elegant
scholar. He was well versed in the Fathers, the Schoolmen, and
the learned languages, which were the favorite studies of that
day. (McClure, *op. cit.,*p. 211).
    3.   Thomas Bilson. He was
so complete in divinity, so well skilled in languages, so read in
the Fathers and schoolmen, so judicious in making use of his
readings, that at length he was found to be no longer a soldier,
but a Commander in Chief in the spiritual warfare, especially
when he became a Bishop. (McClure, *Translators Revived*, pp.
215-16).

**III. An Assessment of the Superiority of the Linguistical
Qualifications for Translation of the Translators of the
King James (Authorized) Bible of 1611.** Having read over
some of the foregoing translators who worked on the King James
(Authorized) Bible of 1611, and then looking around during the present
time here in America (or anywhere else in all the world, for that matter),
you can realize the serious lack of genuine scholarship and study in the field
of Biblical Learning--and most especially the Languages of the Bible. Even
in Dean Burgon's day, there were very, very few men who could match up
with the King James Bible Translators. Alexander McClure concluded:

As to the capability of those men, we may say again, that, by the good providence of God, their work was undertaken in a fortunate time. Not only had the English language, that singular compound, then ripened to its full perfection, but the study of Greek, and of the Oriental tongues, and of Rabbinical lore, had then been carried to a greater extent in England than ever before or since. . . . It is confidently expected that the reader of these pages will yield to the conviction, that all the colleges of Great Britain and America, even in this proud day of boastings [about 1857] could not bring together the same number of divines equally qualified by learning and piety for the great undertaking. Few indeed are the living names worthy to be enrolled with those mighty men. It would be impossible to convene out of any one Christian denomination, or out of all, a body of translators, on whom the whole Christian community would bestow such confidence as is reposed upon that illustrious company, or who would prove themselves as deserving of such confidence." (McClure, *Translators Revived*, pp. 63-64).

Need we say anything further about our lack of preparation, at this present time, for any major revision of the Textus Receptus, without which, as Dean Burgon insisted, there should be no major revision of the King James Bible New Testament? We simply must be better prepared for the task in all ways. We must also be willing to take heed to Dean John William Burgon's **WARNINGS** on revision!

INDEX OF CERTAIN WORDS AND PHRASES

About the Author

The author of this book, Dr. D. A. Waite, received a B.A. (Bachelor of Arts) in classical Greek and Latin from the University of Michigan in 1948, a Th.M. (Master of Theology), with high honors, in New Testament Greek Literature and Exegesis from Dallas Theological Seminary in 1952, an M.A. (Master of Arts) in Speech from Southern Methodist University in 1953, a Th.D. (Doctor of Theology), with honors, in Bible Exposition from Dallas Theological Seminary in 1955, and a Ph.D. in Speech from Purdue University in 1961. He holds both New Jersey and Pennsylvania teacher certificates in Greek and Language Arts.

He has been a teacher in the areas of Greek, Hebrew, Bible, Speech, and English for over thirty-five years in nine schools, including one junior high, one senior high, three Bible institutes, two colleges, two universities, and one seminary. He served his country as a Navy Chaplain for five years on active duty; pastored two churches; was Chairman and Director of the Radio and Audio-Film Commission of the American Council of Christian Churches; since 1971, has been Founder, President, and Director of THE BIBLE FOR TODAY; since 1978, has been President of the DEAN BURGON SOCIETY; has produced over 700 other studies, books, cassettes, or VCR's on various topics; and is heard on both a five-minute daily and thirty-minute weekly radio program IN DEFENSE OF TRADITIONAL BIBLE TEXTS, presently on 25 stations. Dr. and Mrs. Waite have been married since 1948; they have four sons, one daughter, and, at present, eight grand-children.

 Defending the King James Bible--by Dr. D. A. Waite; 352 pp. hardback.; a four-fold superiority of the KJB is given: Superior TEXTS, TRANS-LATORS, TECHNIQUE, and THEO-LOGY. 251 review questions in the appendix plus a listing of all the complete English Bibles and New Testaments since 1300. 5th printing.
☐ BFT #1594-P @ $12.00

 Four Reasons for Defending the King James Bible--by Dr. D. A. Waite. 28 pp. This is a brief summary of the KJB's superior texts, translators, technique, and theology elaborated upon in *Defending the King James Bible*. Reference is made to the larger book for more details on each point.
☐ BFT #2423 @ $2.00

 The Revision Revised--by Dean John William Burgon, 640 pp. hard-back; a beautifully printed book, in which Dean Burgon does four things: (1) He attacks the false Greek text of Westcott and Hort; (2) He demolishes the theory behind that text; (3) He refutes the E.R.V. of 1881 and (4) He defends the King James Bible!
☐ BFT #611 @ $25.00

 Westcott & Hort's Greek Text & Theory Refuted--by Dr. D. A. Waite, 36 pp., a summary from Dean Burgon's *Revision Revised* of the serious defects both in Westcott and Hort's Greek text as well as the false and unfounded theory on which that false text was based. Reference is made extensively to the larger book.
☐ BFT #2695 @ $3.00

 The Last Twelve Verses of Mark--by Dean John William Burgon, 400 pp., perfect bound, with powerful and convincing documentation. Dean Burgon vindicates and establishes Mark 16:9-20 as genuine. In his day, the only manuscripts (with few exceptions) that omitted these verses were the false Vatican & Sinai MSS.
☐ BFT #1139 @ $15.00

 Dean Burgon's Vindication of the Last Twelve Verses of Mark--by Dr. D. A. Waite, 36 pp.; a summary of Dean Burgon's *Last Twelve Verses of Mark*. The extensive arguments of Dean Burgon are placed in easy to follow chart and table form so that the abundant proof in favor of these verses can be easily seen.
☐ BFT #2506 @ $3.00

 The Traditional Text of the Holy Gospels--by Dean John William Burgon, 384 pp. hardback. A careful survey of the historical supremacy of the N.T. Greek text that has been preserved from the first century until the present. Dean Burgon shows the superiority of this text and the inferiority of B and Aleph and others.
☐ BFT #1159 @ $16.00

 A Brief Summary of Dean Burgon's *Traditional Text of the Holy Gospels*--by Dr. D. A. Waite, 36 pp., a brief summary of the major arguments of Dean Burgon's book, *The Traditional Text*, outlining his seven tests of truth, the superiority of the traditional text, and the inferiority of the Westcott & Hort N.T. text.
☐ BFT #2771 @ $3.00

 The Causes of Corruption of the Traditional Text--by Dean John William Burgon, 360 pp. hardback; detailed illustrations of five accidental causes and ten intentional causes of the corruption of the original traditional text. The book is replete with condemnation of the B/Aleph, Vatican/Sinai & Westcott and Hort N.T. Greek text.
☐ BFT #1160 @ $15.00

 A Brief Summary of the Causes of the Corruption of the Traditional Text--by Dr. D. A. Waite, 40 pp.; a brief summary of Dean Burgon's *Causes of Corruption*, illustrating briefly the five causes of accidental corruption and the ten causes of intentional corruption of the original traditional text.
☐ BFT #2780 @ $3.00

☐ **BFT #2764VC1-4 @ $45.00--FOUR, 6-hour Videos**
King James Bible Seminar Videos--420 Transparencies

Foes of the King James Bible Refuted--by Dr. D. A. Waite , 158 pp.; a refutation of six leading foes of the KJB taken from the television script of the John Ankerberg program. The arguments are as old as the Westcott and Hort errors. They deserve clear answers and receive them in this booklet.

☐ BFT #2777 @ $9.00

The Comparative Readability of the Authorized Version--by Mr. D. A. Waite, Jr., 84 pp.; an objective, computer generated comparison of the readability of seven versions: KJB, ASV, RSV, NASV, NIV, NKJV, & NRSV. The King James Bible wins in readability in most categories based on current readability formulas.

☐ BFT #2671 @ $5.00

The Theological Heresies of Westcott and Hort--by Dr. D. A. Waite, 52 pp.; 125 direct quotations from three of Bishop Westcott's books and two of Professor Hort's books, showing their apostasy in all ten areas of theological thought. Don't believe those who tell you they were "conservative" theologians!

☐ BFT #595 @ $3.00

Bishop B. F. Westcott's Clever Denial of Christ's Bodily Resurrection--by Dr. D. A. Waite, 56 pp.; an analysis of two of Westcott's books on the resurrection of Christ showing clearly his heretical denial of Christ's **bodily** resurrection. He also denies Christ's **bodily** ascension and **bodily** second coming. Beware!

☐ BFT #1131 @ $4.00

Dean Burgon's Confidence in the King James Bible-- by Dr. D. A. Waite, 36 pp.; an answer to the lie of James White that Dean Burgon would not use ONLY the King James Bible. The booklet is replete with quotations from Dean Burgon's *Revision Revised* in which he defends the KJB forcefully and accurately!

☐ BFT #2591 @ $3.00

The Paraphrased Perversion of the Bible--Analysis of the Living Version N.T. by Dr. Gene Nowlin, 344 pp. perfect bound; a detailed analysis from a theological and translational standpoint of the *Living Version New Testament*. This should be given to those who still think there is spiritual value in the LV.

☐ BFT #127 @ $6.00

A Brief Analysis of the NIV Inclusive Language Edition ("NI-VILE")--by Dr. D. A. Waite, 56 pp.; In spite of the plan of the NIV to go gender-inclusive and then the withdrawl of that plan, the NIV has published in England such an edition. 136 examples of faithless treatment of God's Words are given!

☐ BFT #2768 @ $4.00

The Contemporary English Version (CEV), An Antichrist Version (ACV)?--by Dr. D. A. Waite, 34 pp.; The latest perversion from the American Bible Society is analyzed and condemned. 29 doctrinal words and 22 other important words have been dropped out of this CEV. Destined to be the pattern for the world!

☐ BFT #2721 @ $3.00

The Case for the King James Bible, A Summary of the Evidence and Argument--by Dr. D. A. Waite, 96 pp.; this booklet is a brief summary from three different books of the favorable evidence for the Hebrew and Greek texts that underlie the King James Bible. An updated edition of the author's 1971 work.

☐ BFT #83 @ $7.00

The Textus Receptus Greek New Testament Underlying the KJB-- printed by The Trinitarian Bible Society, 487 pp.; this is a reprint of Dr. Frederick Scrivener's Greek text which exactly underlies the King James Bible. It is based on Beza's 5th edition of 1598 and should be the basis for any New Testament translation in any language.

☐ BFT #471 @ $14.00

Get our NEW BOOK on *Foes of the KJB Refuted*--$9.00!!

Order Blank (p. 1)

Name:_____

Address:_____

City & State:_____Zip:_____

Credit Card #:_____Expires:_____

[ ] Send *Burgon's Warnings on Revision* by DAW ($7+$3 S&H) A perfect bound book, 120 pages in length.

[ ] Send *The Case for the King James Bible* by DAW ($7 +S&H) A perfect bound book, 112 pages in length.

[ ] Send *Foes of the King James Bible Refuted* by DAW ($9 +$4 S&H) A perfect bound book, 164 pages in length.

[ ] Send *The Revision Revised* by Dean Burgon ($25 + $4) A hardback book, 640 pages in length.

[ ] Send *The Last 12 Verses of Mark* by Dean Burgon ($15+$4) A perfect bound paperback book 400 pages in length.

[ ] Send *The Traditional Text* hardback by Burgon ($16 + $4) A hardback book, 384 pages in length.

[ ] Send *Summary of Traditional Text* by Dr. Waite ($3 + $2)

[ ] Send *Summary of Causes of Corruption*, DAW ($3+2 S&H)

[ ] Send *Causes of Corruption* hardback by Burgon ($15 + $4) A hardback book, 360 pages in length.

[ ] Send *Inspiration and Interpretation*, Dean Burgon ($25+$4)

[ ]Send *Contemporary Eng. Version Exposed*, DAW ($3+$2)

Send or Call Orders to:
THE BIBLE FOR TODAY
900 Park Ave., Collingswood, NJ 08108
Phone: 609-854-4452; FAX:--2464; Orders: 1-800 JOHN 10:9
E-Mail Orders: BFT@BibleForToday.org; Credit Cards OK

Order Blank (p. 2)

Name:_____

Address:_____

City & State:_____Zip:_____

Credit Card#:_____Expires:_____

Other Materials on the KJB & T.R.

[ ] Send *Westcott & Hort's Greek Text & Theory Refuted by Burgon's Revision Revised—Summarized* by Dr. D. A. Waite ($4.00 + $3 S&H)

[ ] Send *Defending the King James Bible* by Dr.Waite $12+$4 A hardback book, indexed with study questions.

[ ] Send *Guide to Textual Criticism* by Edward Miller ($7 + $4)

[ ] Send *Westcott's Denial of Resurrection*, Dr. Waite ($4+$3)

[ ] Send *Four Reasons for Defending KJB* by DAW ($2+$3)

[ ] Send *Vindicating Mark 16:9-20* by Dr. Waite ($3 + $3)

[ ] Send *Dean Burgon's Confidence in KJB* by DAW ($3+$3)

[ ] Send *Readability of A.V. (KJB)* by D. A. Waite, Jr. ($5 +$3)

[ ] Send *NIV Inclusive Language Exposed* by DAW ($4+$3)

[ ] Send *23 Hours of KJB Seminar* (4 videos) by DAW ($50.00)

[ ] Send *Defined King James Bible* lg.prt. leather ($40+S&H)

[ ] Send the "DBS Articles of Faith & Organization" (N.C.)
[ ] Send Brochure #1: "1000 Titles Defending KJB/TR"(N.C.)
Send or Call Orders to:
THE BIBLE FOR TODAY
900 Park Ave., Collingswood, NJ 08108
Phone: 609-854-4452; FAX:--2464; Orders: 1-800 JOHN 10:9
E-Mail Orders: BFT@BibleForToday.org; Credit Cards OK

Order Blank (p. 3)

Name:_____

Address:_____

City & State:_____Zip:_____

Credit Card#:_____Expires:_____

More Materials on the KJB &T.R.

[ ] Send *Heresies of Westcott & Hort* by Dr. Waite ($4+$3)

[ ] Send *Scrtvener's Greek New Testament Underlying the King James Bible*, hardback, $14+$4 S&H

[ ] Send *Why Not the King James Bible?--An Answer to James White's KJVO Book* by Dr. K. D. DiVietro, $9+$4 S&H

[ ] Send *Forever Settled--Bible Documents & History Survey* by Dr. Jack Moorman, $21+$4 S&H

[ ] Send *Early Church Fathers & the A.V.--A Demonstration* by Dr. Jack Moorman, $6 + $4 S&H.

[ ] Send *When the KJB Departs from the So-Called "Majority Text"* by Dr. Jack Moorman, $16 + $4 S&H

[ ] Send *Missing in Modern Bibles--Nestle-Aland & NIV Errors* by Dr. Jack Moorman, $8 + $4 S&H

[ ] Send *The Doctrinal Heart of the Bible--Removed from Modern Versions* by Dr. Jack Moorman, VCR, $15 +$4 S&H

[ ] Send *Modern Bibles--The Dark Secret* by Dr. Jack Moorman, $3 + $2 S&H

[ ] Send *Early Manuscripts and the A.V.--A Closer Look*, by Dr. Jack Moorman, $15 + $4 S&H

Send or Call Orders to:
THE BIBLE FOR TODAY
900 Park Ave., Collingswood, NJ 08108
Phone: 609-854-4452; FAX:--2464; Orders: 1-800 JOHN 10:9
E-Mail Orders: BFT@BibleForToday.org; Credit Cards OK

the
**BIBLE
FOR
TODAY**
900 Park Avenue
Collingswood, NJ 08108
Phone: 609-854-4452

B.F.T. #804